Dreams From My Mother

A Story of Race, Cultures, and Hope

Christian Guerrier

Lucas:
We have a lot of work to do to heal ourselves & the world

07/17/23

Dedication

This book is dedicated to all women and children living under military dictatorships in their native land or colonized territories around the world. May they put all their faith in God and renew it at sunrise every day. May God speed the day of Universal Freedom and collective healing.

I want to thank my editors: Anita Francois and Adrienne Horn for helping me bring this story to the world. I also want to acknowledge the following list of warrior women whose words and writings have taught me, raised my awareness and prepared me to be part of their big celebration in 2020.

Oprah Winfrey, Assata Shakur, Marianne Williamson, Toni Morrison, Angela Davis, Ida B. Wells, Edwige Danticat, Marleine Bastien, Mother Jones, Anaïs Nin, Fabienne Claude, Marlene Daut, Sherri Mitchell, Wena'hamu'gwasit and Bayyinah Bello.

"Aspiring to the glory that comes from being a man of letters is not the reason I write; my goal is to be of use to my compatriots, to enlighten them, and to unveil the truth to Europeans." - Baron De Vastey, Haytian Historian, (Oct 1814)

Le serment des ancêtres. This 1822 painting by the Guadeloupean painter Guillaume Guillon Lethière, representing Alexandre Pétion and Jean-Jacques Dessalines, was housed in Haiti's presidential palace until it was damaged during the 2010 earthquake. Public domain via Wikimedia Commons.

Introduction

LIBERTY OR DEATH.
INDIGENOUS ARMY,

TODAY, January first, eighteen hundred and four, the General in Chief of the Indigenous army, accompanied by the Generals, Chiefs of the army, who were summoned in order to take the measures that will ensure the welfare of the country.

After having made known to the assembled Generals, his true intentions, which are to assure forever a stable Government for the Indigenous of Hayti, his primary objective; which he did in a speech that has been made known to Foreign Powers, his resolution to make the country independent, and to enjoy a liberty consecrated by the blood of the inhabitants of this Island; and after having taken their advice, has asked that each of the assembled Generals take an oath to renounce France forever, to die rather than live under its dominion, and to fight for independence until their last breath.

The Generals, deeply moved by these sacred principles, after having given with a unanimous voice their adherence to the clearly stated project of independence, have all sworn to posterity, to the whole universe, to renounce France forever, and to die rather than live under its dominion.

Done at Gonaïves, this 1st of January 1804 and the 1st. day of the independence of Hayti.

Signed,

J.J. DESSALINES, General in chief; Christophe, Pétion, Clervaux, Geffrard, Vernet, Gabart, Division Generals; P. Romain, E. G[é]rin, F. Capoix, Daut, Jean-Louis-Francois, F[é]rou, Cangé, L. Bazelais, Magloire Ambroise, J. Jques. Herne, Toussaint Brave, Yayou, Brigadier Generals ; Bonnet, F. Papalier, Morelly, Chevalier, Marion, Adjustant Generals; Magny, Roux, Chiefs of Brigade, Char[é] ron, B. Loret, Quené, Makajoux, Dupuy, Carbonne, Diaquoi aîné, Raphaël, Malet, Derenoncourt, Officers of the army, and Boisrond Tonnerre, Secretary

THE GENERAL IN CHIEF, TO THE PEOPLE OF HAYTI
CITIZENS,

IT is not enough to have expelled from your country the barbarians who have bloodied it for two centuries; it is not enough to have put an end to those resurgent factions that one after another mocked the phantom of liberty which France exposed to our eyes; it is necessary by a last act of national authority, to forever ensure the empire of liberty in the country that gave us birth; we must seize from the inhuman government that has for a long time kept us in the most humiliating torpor, all hope of re-enslaving us; we must then live independent or die.

Independence, or death… let these sacred words unite us, and let them be the signal of battle, and of our reunion.

Citizens, my Countrymen, I have assembled on this solemn day those courageous soldiers, who, as liberty lay dying, have spilled their blood to save her; these Generals who have guided your efforts against tyranny, have not yet done enough for your happiness… the French name still haunts our country.

Everything there recalls the memory of the cruelties of those barbarous people; our laws, our manners, our towns, everything still carries the imprint of the French; what do I say, there are Frenchmen in our Island, and yet you think you are free and independent of that Republic which fought every other nation, it is true; but which has never vanquished those who are determined to be free.

What! victims for fourteen years of our credulity and indulgence; vanquished, not by French armies, but by the misleading eloquence of their agents' proclamations; when will we be tired of breathing the same air as they do? What do we have in common with these executioners? Their cruelty compared to our patient moderation; their color with ours, the vast expense of the seas that separate us, our avenging climate, all tell us that they are not our brothers, that they will never be, and that if they find asylum among us, they will again be the instigators of our troubles and our divisions.

Native Citizens, men, women, girls, and children, cast your gaze on every part of this Island, look for your wives, your husbands, your brothers, and your sisters; what do I say, look for your children, your suckling babies? What has become of them… I shudder to say it…the prey of these vultures. Instead of these precious victims, your saddened eye only sees their assassins; these tigers still covered with their blood, and whose atrocious presence reproaches your insensitivity and your culpable slowness in avenging them. What are you waiting for before appeasing their spirits; remember that you want your remains to rest near those of your fathers when you have driven tyranny out; will you descend into their tombs without having avenged them? No, their bones would repulse yours.

And you precious men, intrepid Generals who, without concern for your own misfortunes, have resuscitated liberty by giving her all your blood; know that you have accomplished nothing, unless you give to the nations a terrible, but just, example of the vengeance that must be wrought by a nation proud of having recovered its liberty, and jealous of maintaining it; let us frighten all those who would dare to try to take it from us again: let us begin with France… Let them shudder when they approach our coasts, if not from the memory of the cruelties they perpetrated there, then by the terrible resolution that we shall enter into of putting to death, anyone who is born French, and who would soil with their sacrilegious foot the territory of liberty.

We have dared to be free, let us dare to be so by ourselves and for ourselves; let us imitate the growing child: his own weight breaks the bassinet that has become useless to him and that shackles him in his march. What people fought for us? What nation would reap the fruits of our labors? And what dishonorable absurdity it would be having vanquished to become slaves. Slaves... Let us leave that epithet to the French; they have won, only to lose their freedom.

Let us walk in other footsteps, let us imitate those nations who, carrying their solicitude all the way to the future and not willing to leave an example of cowardice for posterity, have preferred to be exterminated rather than to lose their place as on the list of free nations.

Let us ensure however that a proselytizing spirit does not destroy our work; let our neighbors breathe in peace, let them live quietly under the aegis of the laws that they have made for themselves, and let us not go, as revolutionary firebrands proclaiming ourselves legislators of the Antilles, seek glory by disturbing the tranquility of the neighboring Islands; they have not, like the one that we inhabit, been drenched with the innocent blood of their inhabitants; they have no vengeance to claim from the authority that protects them.

Fortunate to have never known the scourges that have destroyed us; they can only wish for our welfare.

Peace to our neighbors, but anathema to the French name, eternal hatred to France: that is our cry.

Natives of Hayti! My happy destiny was to be one day the sentinel who is to guard the idol to which you sacrifice: I have watched, fought, sometimes alone; and if I have been so fortunate to deliver to you the sacred charge you entrusted to my care, remember that it is now your turn to preserve it. In fighting for your liberty, I have labored for my own happiness. Before consolidating it by laws that ensure your individual liberty, your Chiefs, whom I am assembling here, and I, owe you the last proof of our devotion.

Generals and you Chiefs gathered here with me for the happiness of our country, the day has arrived, this day will eternalize our glory, our independence.

Should a cool heart be amongst you, let him drawback, and tremble at the thought of pronouncing the oath that is to unite us.

Let us swear before the whole universe, to posterity, to ourselves to renounce France forever, and to die rather than live under its dominion.

To fight until our last breath for the independence of our country.

And you, people that have too long been unfortunate, witness the oath that we are taking, remember that I have counted on your fidelity and courage when I entered the pursuit of liberty to fight the despotism and the tyranny against which you had struggled for fourteen years; remember that I have sacrificed everything to fly to your defense, parents, children, fortune, and now I am rich only in your liberty; that my name has become a horror to all those who want slavery, and that despots and tyrants never utter it unless to curse the day that I was born; and if you ever refused or muttered while receiving the laws that the spirit that watches over your destinies, shall dictates to me for your happiness, you would deserve the fate of ungrateful people.

But I reject this shocking idea; you will be the support of the liberty you cherish, the support of the chief who commands you.

Swear then to live free and independent, and to prefer death to anything that will try to place you back under the yoke. Swear, at last, to pursue forever the traitors and the enemies of your independence.

DONE *at the Headquarters at Gonaives, the first January, eighteen hundred and four, the first year of independence.*

Signed,

J. J. DESSALINES

IN THE NAME OF THE PEOPLE OF HAYTI,

WE the Generals in Chief of the Armies of the Island of Hayti, penetrated with gratitude toward the benefits, we have experienced by the General in Chief, Jean Jacques Dessalines, the protector of the liberty which the nation enjoys.

In the name of liberty, in the name of independence, in the name of the people he has made happy, we proclaim him Governor-General, for life, of Hayti; we swear to blindly obey the Laws issued by his authority, the only one we acknowledge: we give him power to make peace, war, and to name his successor.

Done at the headquarters of Gonaives, this 1st of January 1804, and the first day of independence.

Signed,

Gabart, P. Romain, J. Herne, Capoix, Christophe, Geffrard, E. G[é]rin, Vernet, Pétion, Clervaux, Jean-Louis-Francois, Cangé, F[é]rou, Yayou, Touissant Brave, Magloire Ambroise, Louis Bazelais.

Chapter 1

Hayti

"To write our declaration of independence, we should have the skin of a white man for parchment, his skull for an inkwell, his blood for ink, and a bayonet for a playpen." - Adjacent General Boisrond Tonnerre, principal author of Hayti's Declaration of Independence, 1804.

"Never again shall a colonist, or a European set his foot upon this territory with the title of master or proprietor." - General -in-Chief Jean-Jacques Dessalines, Hayti's liberator, April 28, 1804

My story begins in Hayti, spelled in the Modern Era as *Haiti*. The island is popularly known ONLY as the poorest nation in the Western Hemisphere. The European colonizers invented this narrative in the mid-20th century to diminish the glorious contributions of Hayti to universal human rights and equality. Hayti is the only country in the New World which was established on the extermination of European colonists. The Haitian heroes made sure that the myth of white male superiority was totally debunked after the defeat of the European Army on November 18, 1803, and the white establishment has never forgiven Hayti for that. This same establishment has been planning and plotting secretly for the destruction of Hayti since the magnanimous Jean-Jacques Dessalines, the most defamed hero of the revolution, declared a perpetual war on January 1, 1804 against the European colonizers, a people whom he described as "true cannibals" and the natural enemies of black and brown people.

The land of Hayti is where I was shaped, molded, and partially raised. I spent the first sixteen formative years of my life living there with my mother and three siblings. We resided in Pont-Rouge, a sacred landmark recorded in world history books as the area upon which emperor Jean-Jacques Dessalines was assassinated. It was there that he left his last footprints and blood on Haytian soil before falling to a trap set by his general, Alexandre Pétion, the founder of the Republic of Haiti.

Before I go into the details about my upbringing, I would like to give a brief synopsis of more than two centuries of history of modern Haiti. Many Haitians have been brainwashed to believe Hayti was founded on January 1, 1804, as a Black Republic. Hayti was neither founded nor established as a Black Republic. Hayti was re-established on January 1, 1804, as a black state and an Indigenous warrior nation. The liberator of Hayti, General Jean-Jacques Dessalines, had a goal to completely decolonize the island from European culture and influence. This is why he said in declaring Hayti's independence from the entire universe, "We have dared to be free. Let us continue free by ourselves and for ourselves." The heroes and heroines of Haiti's independence were pioneers and inventors of universal human rights and freedom. The white world cannot teach the Haytian people anything about human rights and democracy, for white democracy, in the colonial sense, means the oppression of Indigenous people and the enslavement of the children of Africa in the New World. Since the Haytian heroes re-established natural order and beauty in the former French colony, Europeans and colonialists have been writing and telling the history of the Haytian people. Blinded by racial prejudices and greed, they write a version of history that they believe happened, rather than what has actually happened.

Regarding the glorious battle for the freedom and independence of Hayti, there are four heroes and generals, who played a significant role.

The first one is Toussaint L'Ouverture. Though many may have heard him, very few truly understand the depth of his impact in global politics. He was the first black man appointed by the French colonists to govern Saint Domingue, which was known as the richest European colony and jewel of the French empire at that time.

When he emerged on the colonial stage as a soldier, general, and statesman in 1790s, the colony was crumbling. There was a slave uprising in the northern part of the island, a civil rights struggle between the rich Mulatto class and the *Petite-Blancs* (the inferior whites) in the South, and a political division between the French colonists. Half of the French colonists were Republicans, and the other half were Royalists.

Seeing this division with the island, both the Spanish and British crowns attempted to annex the island. The Spanish were triumphant in the East and the British in the North. L'Ouverture outplayed them, expelled them from the island, and regained political control of the colony. By 1797, he was appointed Governor-General for his bravery and cunning leadership by the colonial establishment. He essentially became the Barack Obama of his time.

L'Ouverture's main objective as a political and military leader in the New World was to heal relations between former slaves and slave owners. He returned properties back to the planters who fled the island during the slave uprising and asked them to return to employ and treat the formerly enslaved population as workers. This idea was foreign to the European colonists. They could not conceive the building of a society or civilization without the institution of slavery. As a matter of fact, some of their best thinkers even admitted that slavery was the only system they knew that could perfect the human condition.

According to Hayti's most prominent historian, Baron de Vastey, during Toussaint's administration:

"[There were roughly] 40,000 whites, sub-divided into *Great Planters*, and *Inferior Whites* (*Petite-Blancs*). 30,000 Persons of Colour and Blacks, *nominally free*, likewise sub-divided into *as many sections as there were gradations of complexion more or less approaching white*. 500,000 Black slaves, Natives and Africans, who likewise participated in the colonial prejudices, the *Creoles* separating themselves from the *Africans*; and in these two sub-divisions the domestics, coachmen, and drivers. In all these classes, the same spirit of pride, of arrogance and of vanity, prevailed. The *Great Planters* held the *Inferior Whites* in contempt. These again despised the *People of Colour and Free Blacks*, who in their turn looked down upon their unfortunate brethren in bondage."

As Vastey also noted in his book, An Essay on the Causes of the Revolution and Civil Wars of Hayti, the foundation of the colonial system (white supremacy) was slavery and the prejudice of color.

Toussaint L"Ouverture's vision was for equality among whites and blacks to reign in the colony, a concept that was and still is foreign to Europeans. The constitution he crafted for Saint-Domingue (Hayti's colonial name) in 1801 was at least three centuries ahead of the United States' constitution. This is why Marcus Garvey and many other U.S. abolitionists believe he is the greatest statesman who ever lived and is entitled to the highest stature as a hero among men. As Garvey said, "… [Toussaint L"Ouverture] outshone George Washington, Napoleon, and Cromwell as a general and a statesman."

L"Ouverture 's constitution was the most humane and most-read document in the Trans-Atlantic world. The institution of slavery was not only abolished, but it also created an equal playing field for whites and blacks. This was then given to Tobias Lear, the secretary to President Thomas Jefferson on July 4, 1801 (U.S.' Independence Day) in the partially independent colony to send a message to the New World.

He pioneered the modern commonwealth initiative that governed all Caribbean countries in the Western Hemisphere (except for Hayti and Cuba), such as Jamaica, French Guyana, Trinidad, and Tobago, Bahamas, Barbados, and others. When Toussaint L'Ouverture proposed the idea of what became known as the commonwealth, the colonial establishment rejected it, which resulted in the War of Independence and the Haytian Revolution.

Many scholars confused the Revolutionary War of Independence from France with the Haytian Revolution. The Revolutionary War of Independence from France started as a slave uprising in 1791 and ended on November 19, 1803. However, the Haytian Revolution began almost a year after Toussaint L'Ouverture was captured and martyred in France. He was succeeded by General Jean-Jacques Dessalines, the most ardent avenger of the Haitian revolution and the most defamed black hero in modern history.

White historians wrote extensively about Toussaint L'Ouverture, but very little about Dessalines. The reason is simple. General Dessalines was the man who totally debunked white male superiority and the archaic belief that white lives are more valuable than black lives. In declaring Hayti's freedom and independence on January 1, 1804, he publicly announced the extermination of all French colonialists and the complete decolonization of the land.

On April 28, 1804, after the extermination of the remaining French colonialists, Dessalines told the Colonial world exactly what he felt about them: "...We have returned to these true cannibals war for war, crime for crime, outrage for outrage. Yes, I saved my country. I have avenged America." Throughout the nineteenth and twentieth centuries, he was portrayed as a demon, a black beast, and a monster in novels, journals, and colonial history. A French lieutenant named Armand Levasseur described him as "...a *bossale* [meaning savage] slave from the coast of Africa who did not know how to read and write. He is angry by nature. His face is hideous, and his physiognomy is horrendous." Lastly, a former French planter named H. Furcy de Bremoy's described him as the living incarnation of Satan.

Haitian American scholar Marlene Daut noted in her book *The Tropic of Haiti*:

"...after the transnational circulation of Dessalines's declaration of Haitian independence, several [U.S. American] journals carried a story in which Dessalines was described as a man of 'wild and flighty mind' who killed whites on sight. In this fictional and emotional account, Dessalines captured Toussaint's former master after Toussaint had helped him escape. Toussaint pleaded for his former master's life, but Dessalines replied, 'He must perish because he is white. His color is his guilt.'"

Emperor Jean-Jacques Dessalines is the national hero of Hayti's independence. He is the man the European Army surrendered to on November 19, 1803. Dessalines, born as Jean-Jacques Duclos, was a slave in the French colony of Saint Domingue. He worked on the Duclos plantation until he was 30 years old, and unlike Toussaint, was not a privileged slave. Instead, he was subjected to the harshness and cruelty of being a field slave.

Duclos joined the French colonial army as a soldier shortly after his freedom was purchased by a free black man named Dessalines from whom he adopted his new surname. When Toussaint L'Ouverture became Governor-General of the colony, he appointed him as his principal lieutenant. Like Dr. Martin Luther King Jr. and Malcolm X, Toussaint L'Ouverture and Jean-Jacques Dessalines differed politically from each other in that Toussaint was a natural-born statesman, and Dessalines was a natural-born warrior.

Boisrond-Tonnerre, the author of the Haytian declaration of independence, stated that Dessalines was born for war. To clarify the difference between him and General Toussaint, he wrote that "it was Dessalines alone upon whom the revolutionaries had been relying on the months before the kidnapping of L'Ouverture. We had nothing more to fear from Toussaint L'Ouverture; it was easy to see that he was not the soul of the country's army and that we only looked to Toussaint without Dessalines as the simulacra of a commander in chief."

So why is Dessalines still hated today by the colonial establishment? The answer is simple. Dessalines despised and refused to compromise with the French. The Haitian Revolution, according to him, was about complete decolonization. He re-established Hayti as a black state and an Indigenous warrior nation. As the first ruler of Hayti and the only Emperor of the New World, he outlawed racism and colorism and extended citizenship to all blacks and natives in the Americas. During his campaign of racial extermination, only Polish soldiers who deserted the European Army and German women were spared from the sword.

Dessalines was the pioneer inventor of universal human rights and freedom, which the United Nations eventually adopted post World War II. Unfortunately, a year and ten months after he declared the island an independent Indigenous warrior nation, he was betrayed and assassinated by two of Pétion's generals, Gérin and Yayou. Dessalines died as fearlessly as he lived, surrounded by his comrades in arms. He taught the Haytian people to love liberty more than life itself and that European colonizers, from experience, are their natural enemies. It is because of this fact that he declared eternal war against the Colonial world after the Declaration of Independence was drafted and assigned the black and red flag to the Indigenous army, which symbolizes the black road (Africans) and the red road (Indigenous Americans).

The third and fourth heroes of the Haytian Revolution are General Henry Christophe and Alexandre Pétion. After the fall of Emperor Jean-Jacques Dessalines (Jacques I) on the night of October 17, 1806, a civil war ensued between their followers over the destiny of Hayti. This violent conflict between the monarchical and republican oppositions became known as the Battle of Cibert. On January 1, 1807, the opposing parties came to an agreement to maintain Haytian defenses against the French and established the divisions of the island of Hayti into two governments.

The State of Hayti in the North later became the Kingdom of Hayti under the leadership of Henry Christophe, and the Southwest assumed the title of the Republic of Hayti, modeling after the United States. The plan was to elect a new president every four years to a Senate entrusted with the legislative power. After the death of King Christophe in 1820, the entire island became the Republic of Hayti under the leadership of President Jean-Pierre Boyer. By the entire island, I also mean the eastern portion of Saint Domingue where the Spanish inhabitants identifying themselves as "Dominicans" are today. They ceded from the Republic of Hayti on February 27, 1844 and established what is now known as the Dominican Republic.

The story of the entire island is very rich and complex. Prior to the arrival of the Spanish conquistadors in 1492, the entire island was called Hayti (Ayiti, meaning; the land of mountains) by the Arawak and Tainos, who were the Indigenous people of the land. Hayti was divided into five kingdoms, which were all independent of one another. They were La Maguá, La Marién, Maguana, Xaraguá, and Higuey, respectively. They lived in harmony and beauty with one another. They had no borders nor immigration policies. When Christopher Columbus set foot on Haytian soil on October 12, 1492, he began plotting and planning death and destruction. Columbus described the Indigenous people as a "people full of love and without greed," and he wrote in his diary, "I believe there is no better race or better land in the New World." Less than a few months after, he began murdering them, kidnapping them, and sending them back to Spain to be sold as slaves. He renamed the island Española, meaning little Spain. It is now referred to as Hispaniola.

The Dominican priests, who came with the conquistadors, built the first colonial church, college, and city in the Americas, which they called Santo Domingo (now the capital of the Dominican Republic). When the European colonizers, including the British, French, and Dutch, heard about newfound gold, they settled where modern Hayti is today and fought over territorial control of the land. After growing weary of fighting and killing one another, the King of France and Queen of Spain signed a peace treaty in 1697 that resulted in the island being split in two. The Spanish side was called Santo Domingo, and the French side was called Saint Domingue.

When the black warriors emerged two centuries later, they defeated and expelled the European colonizers from the land and renamed the entire island Hayti (in honor of the Indigenous). The first Haytians were exterminated by the Spanish colonizers, while the second Haytians took an oath on January 1, 1804 to follow the path of their predecessors by choosing extermination rather than bending to the will of the Europeans. This is the briefest and simplest way that I can explain this rich and complex history of the entire island of Hayti (inclusive of present-day Dominican Republic).

I was born on April 5, 1979 in Pétion-Ville, Haiti, a suburbia in the hills of Port-au-Prince, according to my birth certificate. Pétion-Ville was founded in 1831 by mixed-race (mulatto) President Jean-Pierre Boyer to honor his successor Alexandre Sabes Pétion. As mentioned earlier, Pétion and Boyer were the masterminds behind the assassination of Emperor Jean-Jacques Dessalines at Pont-Rouge on the night of October 17, 1806. Despite what my birth certificate states, my mother informed me that I was actually born in Anse-à-Veau, a beautiful and remote commune in southern Haiti, which happens to also be the place where she was born. Completely isolated from the influence of western culture and civilization, she traveled back to Anse-à-Veau specifically for my birth and returned to Pétion-Ville thereafter for work.

Throughout this memoir, I will not use my mother's real name for the sake of her security. To me, she embodies the spirit of the divine black feminine figure of Africa, and for this reason, her name will be

Auset in this story. Auset is the Indigenous name of who the Western World knows today as Isis. Although this is not her birth name, in honor of the divine feminine and Indigenous women all over the world, I will use this name to reference her.

Auset left Anse-à-Veau at twelve years old with her Aunt to seek a better life in the capital city of Port-au-Prince after my grandfather told her that investing in her education was not his top priority. My mother was the only girl of four children, so my grandfather felt that she would have been more useful for cooking and cleaning for her brothers at home. It is enacted in the Haitian constitution that education is a birthright for all Haitian citizens. However, due to more than two centuries of racially-motivated terrorism, military occupations, racist policies, and the strangling of Haiti's economy by France, the United States, Spain, and even Canada, the Haitian government has literally been on its knees begging its enemies for foreign assistance leading to a lack of accessibility for education to *all* Haitian people.

I found out at the tender age of six that my mother didn't know how to read or write. She taught me how to count Haitian gourdes, the currency used by the people of Haiti, and the difference between the Haitian gourdes and the US dollar. "Five gourde equals one U.S. dollar," I remember her saying. While I was learning how to count Haiti's paper currency, she began to tell me about the harshness of her upbringing as a girl and the difficulty of being a woman and a single mother. At that time, I didn't understand what she was telling me and the impacts her words would have in my heart and mind. As I grew into adulthood, I realized she was superhuman. She was the sole breadwinner of the family and made miracles to feed the family and raise four children by working tirelessly almost every day. Looking back at my journey now, I realize that she was not only showing me how to count and work honestly for money, but she was also instilling important values and qualities in me, such as hard work, integrity, personal responsibility, and the power of authenticity.

The class started with pennies and quarters. I'll never forget when she told me in a soft and dignified voice, "Menm si mwen pa konn li ak ekri, mwen pa sòt." This translates to English as "Although I don't know how to read and write, I am not stupid." Those words were like seeds planted in my psyche so they may one day grow and blossom in my journey from innocence to wisdom.

When I became an adult, I realized she was right. Although very important in contemporary society, intelligence is vast and not limited to knowing how to read and write. It was around this time that I first noticed US currency invading the Haitian economy. All of the pennies and quarters I remembered counting were from the United States. She was unconsciously giving me a class on U.S.-Haiti relations and further preparing me for my life's journey, and inevitably, my destiny.

After finding out that her father was not interested in investing in her education at the age of twelve, she decided to leave his house one night for Port-au-Prince. At that time, Port-au-Prince was at the starting point of becoming overpopulated. The brutal U.S. military dictatorship, which ended in 1934, left the country bleeding and wounded. This occupation reopened unhealed wounds left by French colonizers and a legacy of violence that still plagues Haitian society to this day. Franklin Delano Roosevelt said it best as the military occupation came to an end in 1934. "We must constantly provoke the division of the barefoot masses against the oligarchy (or, those living better) and push the Oligarchs to tear each other apart. This is the only way for us to have a continuing predominance of this Negro country that gained its independence in combat, which is a bad example for the 28 million blacks in America."

Bill Clinton followed this exact strategy when he invaded Haiti in 1994. He first sided with the suffering masses and then switched to side with the corrupt ruling elite after he had complete political control of the country. I am not sure what he thought the descendants of the Haitian heroes, which include me, were going to do, knowing that we have a special mission in the world and that we hate tyrants and colonizers. However, he was audacious enough to begin purchasing land in Gonaïves, the sacred commune in Haiti upon which General Jean-Jacques Dessalines stood on January 1st, 1804 to declare eternal war against Europe and the Colonial World.

When I learned that Bill Clinton was a proprietor in Haiti, I thought to myself, *White racism is really a silent and a diabolical long-term agenda.* Franklin D. Roosevelt knew perfectly what he was doing when he amended the article of the Haitian constitution, which previously banned white people from owning land on the island. He knew a cunning politician like Bill Clinton would have emerged, so he paved the way for him and countless other enemies to come as missionaries into Haiti to purchase land almost a century later.

The 1915 U.S. military dictatorship under the administration of Woodrow Wilson did not only pave the way for Clinton's military occupation of Haiti in 1994, but it also set in motion the destruction of the island from within. The mission of Franklin D. Roosevelt and Bill

Clinton was the same - reducing the Haitian people back into slavery. This was something that no power on earth would have been able to accomplish.

By the time my mother arrived in Port-au-Prince in the 1960s, the capital city was already the center of politics, technology, and development. Everything was happening in Port-au-Prince. Anyone who wanted to be photographed anywhere on the island had to go to the capital to do it. Depending on where they were traveling from, they could have spent a minimum of eight to twelve hours by car to get to Port-au-Prince. Mother told me that the road was so bad, it would take her three days to get to Port-au-Prince by car from Anse-à-Veau. Today, it takes only two hours. Most of the roads are still unpaved in Haiti, but compared to 50 years ago, there have been definite improvements.

The warfare the "white world" has waged against the Haitian people in the last 200 years has been purely economic. They made certain to hinder the improvement of the lives of the Haitian people by maintaining control of the government and the economic infrastructure and destabilizing the country. This is one of the main reasons why the local economy is weak today. The farmers cannot bring their goods to the city easily, paved roads are a major challenge to the growth of Haiti's domestic economy, and though there is a lot of food on the island, it's a nightmare for the people to bring them to the markets.

As a child, I remember seeing the pain donkeys and mules often went through - even to the point of collapsing on the roads - to carry salt, corn, and other produce to the local market. I used to feel sad about it, and I still do, because not much has changed in Haiti since then. Various parts of Haiti produce several types of fruits and vegetables. Some areas are known for producing yams, bananas, rice, corn, and other vegetables that are Indigenous to the land; food that often people in the Western World do not eat. Because there has never been political stability in the country, and there aren't enough paved roads or good transportation systems to allow timely travel from the rural areas to the cities, food is often wasted. The people are suffering from hunger in a rich and fertile land.

Prior to the U.S.' occupation of Haiti, there was a beauty on the island and a harmonious spirit among the people. The sacred oath taken by the Haitian warriors in 1804 for the Haitian people to walk in the guidance of the African ancestors and the spirit of the Indigenous people of the Americas was still being honored. The land was clean. There were no plastic bottles or trash being dropped all over the country like we see today. These military invasions and the interdependence of the modern world caused the people to adopt some aspects of the Western World. The Indigenous spirit of the ancestors still guides them, although they are not being led on the Indigenous path. Today, almost everyone in Haiti has a cell phone and a Facebook account. They have access to images and global information in the palm of their hands through their smartphones. They are now all journalists and storytellers. However, they are being led astray. The Clintons installed the current puppet president, and he is leading the people down a very dangerous path.

I have many wonderful memories growing up in Haiti. The government of Haiti has adapted a republic style of government, but the people of Haiti are living the Indigenous way. They are living in the spirit of their ancestors.

I vividly remember myself as a little boy walking with my uncle in Anse-à-Veau. He had a boom box radio perched on his shoulder, although no music was playing. The people were so surprised and in awe of seeing a radio that big that they would gather round to touch it. The radio, to them, looked like an invention out of this world due to Anse-à-Veau being a commune literally uncontaminated by Western culture and technology. Most of the people who lived there had no electricity, no television, and no contact with the outside world. They lived in perfect harmony with nature. The very few inhabitants who had radios owned the smaller kind and are what we would call *the elite of the area*. They also kept up with both national and global politics to inform the residents of the community.

The people were curious to know how many batteries my uncle's radio took because they felt it was too big for one person. I was nine or ten years old at the time. Ever since then, I've paid close attention to the conditions of the people living in rural areas of Haiti, learning from their simple lifestyle and wisdom. I also realized at an early age that rural life was healthier for the people and the environment, whereas city life was a lot more toxic. People living in rural areas were happier, lived longer lives, and were in harmony with Mother Earth and the spirit of the ancestors without the interference of government officials.

Residents of the capital were more aggressive, more French in culture, and more arrogant than the Indigenous African people of Haiti. I believe this is due to the mental colonization of so-called "Haitian leaders" by Catholic institutions controlling the educational system that occurred after the occupation of the U.S. military ended in 1934. These rulers were being taught French literature and ideologies while people of the countryside were reading trees, clouds, rivers, and stars. They possessed an ancestral knowledge and wisdom of the land that those in charge were disconnected from. They knew the names of every medicinal plant and types of soil for growing food, but those living in Port-au-Prince (dependent on them for food) would look down upon them. They were called "nèg mòn" by the "intellectuals," which is synonymous with being called ignorant and uncivilized.

My spirit was much happier outside of the city. I was always disgusted by the state-sponsored violence and gut-wrenching poverty that affected people living in the slums of Port-au-Prince. However, it was part of God's plan for me to reside there and gain the insight and perspective that I would later need for my journey. I unconsciously made the best of my days there as a teenager, learning the lessons that were meant for my spirit to mature. In the back of my mind, I have always wanted to make a difference in the lives of marginalized people.

My grandmother passed away when my mother was ten years old. Unfortunately, due to the rarity of photographs being taken outside of civilization (Port-au-Prince), my family does not own a photograph of her. Not much has changed for the people in her community since she passed away more than a decade ago. I will never know what she looked like or anything about her life other than what my mother could remember since there is no record of her existence. She disappeared from us like smoke in the sky, similar to many of our enslaved ancestors. This lack of recordkeeping is still common among many families in parts of the island today, who have no choice but to maintain the Indigenous way of living.

When you live inside a bubble like the United States, you tend to forget about the crude reality most members of our human family are subjected to around the world. You often form the habit of looking at distant relatives through the lens of the oppressor and unconsciously join or support them in their mission of colonization. They taught us to hate the oppressed and the poor, and we no longer see them holistically. Many of us believe that their condition of living is a direct result of their ignorance and laziness. We fail to realize that what affects one member of the human family, in fact, impacts all children of the earth. This is Indigenous knowledge that we have been starved of.

We forget that Indigenous people around the world, including those within the United States and Canada, do not live in comfort and luxury. Many of them are living in similar conditions with our brothers and sisters in the developing world. Few people know that there are Native

American tribes in the United States that have been without running water for almost a century. European descendants in the Americas have no clue how deadly colonization has been or how it has affected Indigenous people worldwide. They have no idea. They see suffering and death in other parts of the world as a natural phenomenon, or as Charles Darwin explains in his theory of evolution, "...at some future period, not very distant as measured by centuries, the civilized races of man will almost certainly exterminate and replace throughout the world the savage races." The civilized races of man that Darwin is referring to are the Europeans, and the savages are apparently the Indigenous people. Both the colonizers and the colonized are programmed to be apathetic towards one another, not knowing that their way of thinking and living, which are interchangeable, are responsible for most of the world's suffering and the possible destruction of life on this planet.

We are living in a time where we must restore the natural order, beauty, and harmony on Mother Earth. We, as a collective, can no longer postpone this arduous task for tomorrow and must use the tools endowed upon us to transform the world. We have more power in our hands now than any other generation throughout human history, but we are also more isolated and out of touch than our common ancestors. We are blinded by the material wealth of Western society and spiritually polluted by the culture of excessive consumerism and greed.

I am glad that I am alive at this present moment because this is a glorious time in human history. It is a moment of rebirth and a wonderful opportunity to rebuild the world. Our ancestors prayed and bled for this moment. All we must do now is work on becoming our true selves. Many of us are still afraid to take off the mask of survival that the colonizers have given us. However, it will fall off eventually.

Let me return to my mother's story before I go off on another tangent. When my mother arrived in Port-au-Prince in the early '60s, her aunt brought her to an upper-class Haitian family where she begins to work as a *restavèk* for most of her teenage years. A *restavèk*, deriving from the French language meaning "to stay with," is a domestic servant, who is typically a young girl who cooks and cleans very well. Many people across all socioeconomic classes in Haiti have a *restavèk* working for them.

After the earthquake struck Haiti, I went back to help with the relief efforts, to reconnect with my people, and to share the vision that I had of supporting the education of girls and empowerment of women in the struggle for equality.

While meeting government officials, I came across a middle-class Haitian woman who owned a restaurant in Delmas, an area where the "middle-class" reside. We spoke about the state of women and young girls in Haiti, and as we were becoming more acquainted, she boastfully mentioned her possession of a *restavèk* that she would not trade for the world. She compared the girl to physical property and iterated that "the girl is such an exceptional cook; I don't know what I would do without her in the business." I was shocked to hear these words coming from a woman born in Haiti. However, I didn't want to respond with the words I truly wished to say because I knew that many people, especially the "petty bourgeois" like herself, aspire to live like the corrupt mulatto elite of Haiti. I kept what I was feeling to myself, but I was disgusted. I knew that she was not what the Haitian people would call a *fanm djanm*, meaning an empowered woman. She was a victim of colorism and was subconsciously carrying a lot of pain within her spirit. I recognized the spiritual and emotional damage within her throughout our conversation. I was reminded of how deeply wounded the women in Haiti are and how ingrained the *restavèk* system is in Haitian culture.

It would be almost impossible to change the mindset of the people without complete decolonization of Hayti. In other words, finishing the Haitian revolution. The *restavèk* system, coupled with poverty, is literally the last vestiges of French colonialism and slavery on the island. Young girls whose parents are often too poor to raise them, or in the case of my mother, want more for themselves, travel to Port-au-Prince to stay with a family member or relatives with the hopes of having an education and a better life. Most of the time, they are abused physically, emotionally, and/or sexually. The government fails to protect them, enabling both local and foreign predators to get away with almost anything, including trafficking in the name of charity. The *restavèks* are overworked and often treated with no dignity or respect. The darker the color of a girl's skin, the worst she is treated and abused. It is as William Faulkner stated, "The past is never dead. It's not even past." The most painful part of this is slavery, colorism, and all forms of servitude were outlawed by the Haitian heroes after the expelling and extermination of European colonizers from the land in 1804.

The Haitian ancestors left sacred documents to guide us towards our healing. They warned us that if we ever see a white man in Haiti with a gun, the whole island needs to unite and be ready for war because of the atrocious crimes they had committed on their arrival to the continent. The ancestors wrote in detail on the horrors of slavery and the humiliating and painful experiences of living under European domination.

Black and mulatto women were subjected to the worst form of abuse. Baron de Vastey expressed this in one of his most popular books published in 1814, *Le Système colonial dévoilé*

"Haitian women were at the mercy of these lewd men, who abused them in the most horrific manner imaginable. I shudder when I think of the number of doomed victims sacrificed to these jealous rages: on mere suspicion, they would be whipped or flayed alive; those who put up any resistance to the lustful passion of these men would be made to suffer the most excruciating torment before dying. The woman might be married or living with a black man, or she might be an innocent young girl still under her mother's wing: the colonists in his immorality made no distinction, he stopped at nothing. This arrogant master violated all of nature's laws, ruthlessly and without remorse; death was the punishment for anyone who attempted to place an obstacle between the master and his passions by daring to cry out. Men saw their wives dragged away, and they could only watch in silence; mothers saw their daughters ripped from their arms, and they could not say a word of complaint to anyone in the face of such excessive brutality and injustice."

Many books and documents were taken out of Haiti's cultural archives after the U.S. occupation of Haiti ended in 1934. The partial goal of the occupation was to erase the memory of the Haitian people and to colonize their minds. Abused young girls being subjected to the *restav*èk system in Haiti, is a chapter right out of the colonial era. The institution of slavery and color prejudices were the glue that kept the plantation economy together. Today, in the age of global capitalism and colonial patriarchy; the same colonial strategy is used to keep people oppressed.

My mother's experiences as a *restav*èk are different in comparison to the realities of girls trapped in the system today not only because the economic and political conditions of the country have worsened but also because she was getting paid for her labor. Nowadays, they are not getting paid. According to my mother's account, she was treated well by the family she was working for. Her salary started at seven gourdes a month, and three months later, it was raised to twelve gourdes. She worked there until she was able to save enough money to start a small business selling cooking oil and other basic food items.

From the day I became consciously aware of myself and my environment, I remembered my beloved mother always working and building her business. She is a natural entrepreneur in spirit, always observing and adapting to the Haitian market economy despite what was going on in the country politically. If there was a system in place for the development of small businesses and a government that was looking out for the interest of its people, she would have been very successful financially and would have contributed significantly to the economic growth of the country. But instead, she has been suppressed to become like the rest of the women and girls on the island - a victim of global patriarchy and corruption.

My mother is in my prayers every day when I think about the deadly plight the enemies of humanity, meaning those who believe in the ideology of racial separation, set forth for the Haitian people. I pray every moment that she is protected from harm due to the current political climate of the country. The foreign enemies are fueling division and violence, too many innocent people are being killed, and the world is not paying attention. I want to be a son that she can be proud of and fulfill the promise I made to her when I was thirteen of buying her a home. Throughout life, I have observed Ausset endure pain and suffering both as a woman and a mother. She deserves to live and be treated like the modern queen of Haiti, and I am going to fight tooth and nail to make it happen.

Her story sparked my curiosity in a very unique way, broadened my circle of empathy for all women and mothers around the world, and steered me onto the path of becoming a champion for women in the United States, and soon, around the world. I believed that the discrimination my mother experienced as a girl was just an isolated and unfortunate experience due to my grandfather living entirely outside of modernity as a farmer and not knowing any better. The older and more mature I become, I realize that gender discrimination is more problematic and deadly than I thought. Discrimination against women is a worldwide and historical issue that has handicapped the human race.

The oppression of women began with the onset of colonization. Evolutionary biologist Patricia Adair Gowaty was absolutely right when she stated, "Women's oppression is the first, most widespread, and deepest oppression." During a sacred ceremony, Wayne Snellgrove from the *Saulteaux* tribe in Northern Canada shared that when the Europeans first came to his tribe, they asked to speak with the ones in charge. The warriors introduced them to the mothers and grandmothers, and the European colonizers laughed in disbelief that women were regarded with that much esteem to govern the tribes. In the colonial context, the essence of domination is masculinity. Ever since then, a system of male chiefdom implemented by colonialists reversed the natural order of his

Indigenous tribe. The mothers and the grandmothers were no longer in charge, and the lives of the people have not been the same.

Evolutionary biologist Patricia Adair Gawaty said, "Sexist oppression is fundamental to the root of all other systems of oppression." It's almost impossible to solve the current global challenges that we have inherited from previous generations without smashing colonial patriarchy. In the world today, there are more than 90 million girls in developing countries who are not enrolled in school simply because of their gender. When you think about this statistic, it's only right to ask yourself what the role of UNICEF, the World Bank, and the United Nations are. Were they erected after World War II to recolonize black and brown nations? This is not clear, but as far as I'm concerned, since these entities have been in Haiti, their presence has been akin to colonialism. They have installed their own leader, undermined Haitian democracy, and infected the water supply with cholera leading to over 10,000 deaths of innocent men, women, and children.

Since March 31, 1995, the UN so-called "peacekeeping" troops have been in Haiti in the name of upholding democracy. They charge the Haitian government some 66 million dollars a year for security yet have not built one school nor hospital for the people.

All they do is drive around in air-conditioned cars, enjoy the beautiful beaches, and rape Haitian women and children. Out of the 90 million girls around the world who are not enrolled in school, there are more than 300,000 of them in Haiti. The status quo has shown thus far that these entities do not care about the state of women and girls in the world. Their spirits and hearts are too hardened.

In countries like India and China, gender discrimination is even more lethal. According to Steven Pinker, the author of *The Better Angels of Our Nature*, "In China midwives kept a bucket of water at the bedside to drown the baby if it was a girl." In India, they were known for "giving a pill of tobacco and bhang to swallow, drowning in milk, smearing the mother's breast with opium or the juice of the poisonous Datura, or covering the child's mouth with plaster of cow-dung before it drew breath. Then and now, even when the daughters are suffered to live, they may not last long." Steven Pinker continues, "Parents allocate most of the available food to their sons. A Chinese doctor explains, "If a boy gets sick, the parents may send him to the hospital at once, but if a girl gets sick, the parents may say to themselves, 'Well, we'll see how she is tomorrow.'"

The practice of female infanticide is an ancient tradition in China and India, according to some experts. I don't even want to mention countries in Europe because the European continent is marinated in sexism. It is, in my opinion, the cradle of misogyny and women's oppression. The intellectual and cultural tradition of that continent is steeped in hatred for women. Almost all European thinkers were sexists.

Aristotle, one of the most influential thinkers among them, describes women as a mutilated male. He believed women were inferior to men and were comparable to slaves. He mentioned in his book, *Politics*, that "as regards to the sexes, the male is by nature superior and the female inferior, the male ruler and the female subject." Holland Jack also wrote in his book, *The Brief History of Misogyny*, that "the consequences of seeing females as mutilated males could be heard at night, in the world of Classical Antiquity, when newborns' cries disrupted the silence... 'If it is a male, let it live; if it is female, expose it,' wrote Hilarion to his wife, Alis, in 1 BC, testifying to a custom that lasted until Christianity became the dominant religion of the Roman Empire."

Unwanted infants were abandoned in rubbish dumps, the majority of which were baby girls. In some countries in Africa, there is a brutal practice of female genital mutilation that goes back to Arab colonization and enslavement. I guess the point I am making is that the struggle for the emancipation of women is beyond political ideology, racial identity, creed, or individual or national interest. The emancipation and empowerment of women are connected to the healing of the hearts and spirits of men. It's the most important step towards the healing of our beloved Mother Earth. The crimes and injustices committed against women have been going on for too long. Women and girls of all colors have been suppressed, abused, discriminated against, tortured, maimed, and murdered by colonizers in their quest for land, resources, and power for way too long. Time's up for healing and reparation.

We can reverse centuries of crime and abuse if we are fully aware of the time that we are living in. At times we may feel isolated, defeated, or too small to make a difference, but the truth is that half of the battle is already won when we become aware of the problem. There is a saying that once you can identify a problem, you are halfway from solving it. We know that the current social order doesn't work for the human family. We know this system of racial hierarchy is the way of the colonial establishment. American capitalism is a mutation of slavery and European feudalism. It doesn't work well without plundering Indigenous lands and enslaving people for profit.

I am excited to be alive at this moment in history. I hope you are too. Together, we can and must shift this colonial paradigm and usher a new birth of freedom on Earth. This is one of the greatest opportunities we have been bestowed as a people. We must not sleep on it. The time we are living in now is not too different from the time when the Haitian heroes stepped on the world stage and began to decolonize the notion of freedom in the Western Hemisphere. Our task is not as difficult as theirs, but it is a continuation.

The first thing we must do is to start taking responsibility for our individual healing, the healing of our hearts, minds, bodies, and spirits. We are all deeply wounded from our contact with European colonists. As President Obama said, "the worst thing colonialism did was cloud our view of the past." The only country which has successfully overthrown the yoke of European colonialism and charted a new path in the New World is Hayti. The colonial establishment has made an example out of Hayti so that other nations and leaders don't follow or learn from her sharp example. She is being punished every day for daring to be free in a hemisphere conquered by Europeans colonizers.

The process of decolonization is the only hope for the survival of life on our planet. The Colonial world, which I often refer to as the white world, was established on genocide and slavery and sustained by violence. That world is gasping for its last breath. They have lost their hold of the people; they can no longer manipulate us as they used to. The work that we have to do now to make the world better is within us, to re-indigenize our way of life and environment. Governmental leaders will not be able to help us with this process. We have to help, heal, and lead ourselves. We are the ones we've been waiting for.

I am grateful for the sacrifices my ancestors have made on my behalf and Indigenous people around the world. I am who I am today because of them. Sometimes I do feel the task is too big; nevertheless, I never shrink from this ancestral and divine responsibility. Too much is at stake. Our planet is like the Titanic, slowly moving towards an iceberg. The establishment keeps us divided and fighting on superficial issues, such as skin color, while children are starving to die senselessly. The maternal death rate is rising for poor and oppressed women. Fertile lands are being deserted. Hurricanes are getting stronger. Sea levels are rising and will eventually give way to the submerging of lands and the force of millions to migrate inland or to new territories.

We have big challenges to face, and we need to change the course of current events now, but first, we each have to step into our individual responsibility and power. The challenges we are facing cannot and will not be solved with our own intelligence. We will need support and guidance from our Creator. We are finding our way home slowly and surely. Things may seem hopeless on the surface, but deep down, there is a movement of healing taking place silently and privately. Indigenous people are relearning their languages and customs. A new generation of leaders is stepping up to lead from within. Women from the four corners of the globe are coming together to heal, lead, and speak up about the sacredness of all life. Black people in the Americas and Africa are building bonds. Men, young and old, are rejecting the outdated and archaic definition of masculinity.

We are all finding our voices and beginning to use them to raise the awareness and consciousness of our planet. Often, we take the power of our individual voices for granted, although it is the greatest power we have. As we continue exposing injustices and healing generational traumas individually and collectively, we will begin to recreate heaven on Earth. I, for one, am personally committed. My life is now dedicated to helping in this healing process. My mother's story is now my story. Her dreams are now my dreams. Join me on this journey of uncharted territory. I believe wholeheartedly this is why we are alive at this moment in time, witnessing and participating in the next glorious chapter of life on earth. This is the reason I came into this world, to do exactly what my ancestors had done more than two centuries ago - shift this planet into another dimension and elevate it to a higher realm and vibration. Now let's start with how my story began.

* * * * * * * * * * * * * * * * * * * *

I was brought into this world by the beautiful and divine Auset. She met my father in the late 1970s while he was visiting his family in Haiti from the United States. Auset was introduced to my father by a friend. They had a one-night stand, and nine months later, I became an additional male member of the human family. I was given the name of Christian Guerrier, Jr. Christian is a popular western name deriving from Christianity and meaning a follower of Christ. Guerrier means "warrior" in English. I am both a Christian and a warrior in body and spirit. I believe in the power of love and in defending everything that is sacred. In a nutshell, I am a love warrior. Four years after my birth, my mother lost contact with my father. Like most immigrants who are navigating in a world they truly know nothing about, he got caught up trying to survive.

My father's name is Christian Guerrier Sr., a proud man from Port-de-Paix who lives a life of quiet dignity. I met him for the first time when I turned thirteen years old. I was at that age where I was seeking a male role model and yearning to know why he wasn't in my life. The absence of a father in a household does have an impact on the psyche of children. The presence and love of both parents are necessary when raising children in order to do it well. As the renowned African proverb mentions, "It takes a village to raise a child," and this is true. However, the two most important members of that village are the mother and father.

As a boy, I used to dream of my father rescuing me from the brutal poverty I was surrounded by in my community in Pont-Rouge. I didn't know much about him except that he was living in Miami, Florida. My mother didn't own any pictures of him, and in my young mind, I presumed that he had forgotten about his Haitian roots and culture. I believed he was "Americanized" in the colonial sense of the word. In Haiti, I used to hear stories of Haitians who traveled to countries like the United States, Canada, and France, who later forgot about where they came from. I believed my father to be one of those Haitians.

My childhood and most of my teenage years in Haiti were a combination of both joyful and painful memories. Some days were very difficult, and other days were full of light and love. Somehow, they seemed to have been my happiest and most memorable years thus far. I was in both heaven and hell. It was hell because of the racist policies of the Western World towards the island, and heaven because of the hearts of the Haitian people beating in perfect harmony with the ancestors, Mother Earth, and the stars. The whole island is vibrating on different energy, a loving and fulfilling vibration.

I attended Salésians de Don Bosco primary school in Haiti, a colonial project initiated by a priest named Don Bosco for "poor children" around the world after the Vatican had officially recognized Haiti as an independent nation. It seems that this European initiative was designed specifically for Haiti. Today, they are in every formerly colonized territory. The Vatican arrived in Haiti after the nineteenth year of U.S. military occupation ended in 1934 with an invitation from the mixed-race and US.-installed president, Sténio Vincent. As always, the mixed-race individual is the middleman utilized to implement their evil agenda on the island.

I attended Salésians de Don Bosco school because it was free and designed for "poor children." This colonial project is situated in the middle of Lasaline, Pont-Rouge, Cité Soleil, Tokyo, and Cité Militaire, areas that are known as some of the worst slums in Port-au-Prince. Since my journey to the United States in 1996, not much has changed about the school except that there was no yearly tuition. There is a fee for parents to pay, even for the poorest of the poor children to attend.

When I was a student there, I knew something was wrong with the organizational structure of the institution. The white man in charge was a priest from Poland who always looked suspicious and out of touch. His spirit and bodily expressions were always sending opposing messages to my friends and me. As young people, we knew the project was about making money. Since we were isolated from the rest of the world, and we knew we couldn't challenge them because of their control, we went along with the flow.

Since a child, I had always enjoyed watching and observing the priests and other white missionaries in the school. I was curious to know the motivation behind their actions, and why they brought their project to the slums. I do not remember the name of the Priest, but I knew that he was regarded by many people in my community as a good white man. He was always busy and seemed compassionate. His visit was brief, always in and out of the school. He was never comfortable with the students. This is something I have observed on my journey from European people or colonizers when they are involved in the business of exploitation. They are never comfortable in places where there are a lot of Indigenous people. Since many of them do not think and walk in a good way, what they say with their mouth is not what they feel in their hearts. The more aligned an individual is with the spirit, the more discernment he or she will have.

When I was a child in Haiti, I always wondered why almost all the white priests I would see were Polish or German. They were known among the people as the good and merciful whites, at a distance. Since the Catholic priests landed on Haitian soil, they have tried to whitewash Haitian history. They have used their wealth and power to promote their narrative and silence the elders and intellectuals who understood their colonialistic mission. I was not taught in their school that the Haitian people had a history with the Polish and German people that started with the War of Independence from France. It wasn't until I moved to the United States that I began to research and understand this rich and complex history and why Polish priests are selected by the Vatican to run colonial institutions, such as Salésians, like a modern-day plantation on the island.

Now that I can look back at the days I was in that colonial institution, I understand more why most of the priests or "missionaries" behaved the way they did. They were (and still are) wolves in sheep clothing. Their mission is colonizing, exploiting, or enslaving. As the Haitian warriors stated, "they will never change." Deep down in their beings, they knew the school was not about educating, but since these people are so deeply wounded and spiritually impoverished, they have no problem working in the slums under the guise of humanitarians to maintain poverty in Haiti. Many of these Christian missionaries, especially the priests, always seemed uncomfortable and suspicious, and as a wise woman said, "Our faces reveal what's in our heart." Their faces revealed to me that they were the new colonists.

I don't want to go into all the details of the history of the European missionaries in Hayti, but it's important to highlight some aspects of how the German and Polish people were granted Haitian citizenship after the War of Independence from France ended on November 19, 1803. The colonial establishment paints Emperor Jean-Jacques Dessalines in their journals and archives as an exterminator of white people, but history recorded that he was the most magnanimously humane warrior in Modern history. He was the man who invented the term "Universal Human Rights" prior to the Western World after World War II (or second European led world war).

European usurper Napoleon Bonaparte, like his successor Adolf Hilter, had a dream of conquest to build an empire through genocide and slavery in America. To him, empire meant peace. When the Haitian heroes under the leadership of Toussaint L'Ouverture asserted their human rights and charted a new path like the newly independent thirteen colonies in North America (now the U.S.A.), he sent an expedition to commit genocide on the island in 1802. In that expedition, there were 3,000 Polish soldiers and a few men of color. When the Polish soldiers realized that they were fighting to re-enslave the Haitian people, they deserted the French army and joined the Indigenous army under the leadership of General Jean-Jacques Dessalines. After victory was achieved, General Dessalines declared Haiti's independence from France and publicly announced the extermination of the remaining French on the island. The Polish soldiers and German women were spared and granted citizenship under the 1805 Haitian constitution, which classified them as "black."

Shortly after the revolution, the European Governor of Jamaica requested that General Dessalines repatriate the new Haitians to Europe because they were white. General Dessalines' response was that he was the leader of a free and independent people and that "he could not convince Haitian citizens to leave their own country." Today, some of their descendants are now living in an area of Haiti known as Cazale. Almost a century later, before the U.S. occupation of 1915, German businessmen returned to infiltrate Haitian society by marrying into the Haitian elite in order to buy land. The Haitian constitution had formerly forbidden whites to own property, so the return of these German people was in opposition to this rule.

I am stating this only to point out how this history has been haunting Haiti ever since. The white establishment has always used a German or Polish Pope or Priest to run a colonial project in Haiti or to send a political message. Pope Jean-Paul II, who was Polish as well, went to Haiti in 1983 to assert white supremacy by referring to Haiti by its colonial name and diplomatically announcing the ouster of President Jean-Claude Duvalier on Feb 7, 1986. This was the same day Napoleon Bonaparte sent the European expedition to overthrow Toussaint L'Ouverture in 1802.

In Haiti, Europeans have always used a Polish, German, or French man to run a plantation-like project. When Bill Clinton invaded Haiti in 1994, he made sure to bring Polish and Argentinian soldiers with him for the military occupation. They enjoy constantly putting salt on the injuries of Haitians by opening old wounds and inflicting new ones with their silent hatred for the people. As James Baldwin stated; "I imagine one of the reasons people cling to their hates so stubbornly is because they sense, once hate is gone, they will be forced to deal with pain". So, dehumanizing black and brown-skinned people is their way of getting high and is their avoidance of facing the ugliness of their souls.

My life in Haiti forced me to grow older and wiser quickly. I learned early through trial and tribulations more about our world than most adults in developed countries learn at thirty. I met my father for the first time when I was a pre-teen in the late '80s. On that day, I was heading to my school - Salésiens - to eat the tasteless food they served to marginalized children, due to my mother not having any money to feed the family. The feeling of hunger was too painful to bear.

For those who do not know, food is the most effective weapon for the colonizers. It's what they used to bring countries down on their knees and keep people enslaved for so long. The food they served at Salésiens was akin to food for slaves, but, that day, I put my pride aside to eat there, even though I despised the food. As I waited in line, one of the community elders approached to inform me that my father from Florida was at my house looking for me. I became numb. I didn't know what to feel, think, or say at the time. I already succumbed to the excruciating pain of hunger. Hearing my father was in Haiti looking for me was the most unexpected news that I had ever received. At that moment, it was akin to finding out that I had won the Florida lottery. I knew then that my life was going to change for the better.

When I got the news, I left Salésiens right away to meet with him. I was still dealing with hunger, but this new feeling of anxiety quickly took over the pain that I felt in my body. As I walked up to the house, I noticed him standing outside, looking as strong and as confident as I had imagined. Drawing closer, I instantly felt a family connection but was still stoic. I didn't know him, and he felt like a stranger. We had no emotional bonding during this first encounter since I was in the preliminary stages of developing anger towards him for his absence.

Even now, as an adult, I feel a certain distance from my father and people, overall. I find it difficult to connect with people on a superficial level. It doesn't matter if you are family or a complete stranger. My father, like men of his generation, is deeply wounded emotionally and spiritually by the everlasting effects of colonialism. Perhaps this is the reason for the lack of an emotional bond between us still to this day.

As I mentioned at the beginning of my story, Haiti was re-established (not founded) as a black state and Indigenous warrior nation. In many ways, the Haitian people are similar to turtles - tough on the outside and soft on the inside. They are tough because they have been at war with the European world since 1804 and soft because they embody the Indigenous spirit of Africa.

The first question I remember my father asking was, "Are you hungry?" I nodded my head, and he told me to get dressed before we took a taxi to the hotel he stayed in. We ate at a restaurant near his hotel, which was likely the hotel he stayed at when he first met my mother, due to his simple nature. I spent the majority of my time with him listening and observing. He spoke briefly about his life and what had happened between him and my mother. He blamed my mother for losing contact with him, which he claimed to be the reason why he wasn't involved in the early years of my life. He promised me that as soon as he returned to Miami, he would begin working on my immigration papers so that I could join him.

I dreamt of visiting Florida for years, so I was excited to hear that. It didn't take me long to start imagining my life in Miami. Looking at life in the United States from Haiti, Florida was painted as the promised land for dreamers from all walks of life. I have always felt in my heart that I was chosen by destiny to fulfill a divine mission, so instinctively I knew this was the country I needed to be in to reach my potential and have a shot at my dreams.

In Haiti, it felt like I was too isolated and distant from the rest of the world and civilizations. I wasn't in Africa, but at times it felt like I lived in an African country. The only faces I saw were black and being black was the only world that I knew. The correlation between being Haitian and being black was so engrained in my consciousness that anyone who wasn't Haitian wasn't authentically black. Blackness, in the Haitian sense, is a rebellious spirit against colonial oppression or Eurocentric ideals. But blackness, in the colonial sense, is to accept second-class citizenship in a predominantly white society. Haitian people feel they have earned the right to classify a person black or not. Blackness is more than melanin; it is a consciousness and a level of humanity and interconnection. That's why the Polish and German women were classified as black in the 1805 Haitian constitution.

After dinner with my father, he invited me to visit Port-de-Paix the next day - a commune in the Nord-Ouest (North West) region of Haiti - to meet his side of the family. My sister, who was three or four at the time and born in the United States, was also in Haiti with him for the first time. She didn't speak a word of Haitian Creole, nor I of English, so our father acted as the translator for the duration of the trip.

We spent a few days with family in Port-de-Paix. During those days, we stayed at the house of my late Grandmother Izaye, my father's eighty-year-old energetic mother. She was the strongest old woman I had ever met; very agile and full of life. Even at her age, she was, as we say in Haitian Creole, the "poto mitan" (pillar) of the family, looking out for my grandfather who was younger but couldn't even do half of what she capable of. She made sure that we were being taken care of and had everything we needed to make sure our stay was comfortable.

After becoming acquainted with uncles, cousins, and other extended family on my father's side, we drove back to Port-au-Prince. The following day, before flying back to Miami with my sister, my father gave me his phone number on a piece of paper and told me to call any time after 5 p.m. Our communication continued over the phone the following years, but our conversations were always brief. Since there were no cell phones and no internet at the time, I had to walk to a building owned by Tele-Co (a government-owned entity) each time I needed to make a call. After Bill Clinton invaded Haiti, this company became privatized. Today Bill Clinton's close friend, Dennis O'Brien, maintains control of almost all phone calls made in Haiti.

Tele-Co Headquarters was based in Port-au-Prince, Haiti, making it impossible for those located outside of the capital to make calls. Making collect calls via Tele-Co was extremely expensive and the reason why all phone calls were so brief. Costing the same as collect calls being made from incarcerated people to their families in the U.S., this made calling out of Haiti very similar to a prison. If you accepted the call, BellSouth would charge you at least seventy cents per minute. Our world is different today, many millennials and Gen-X do not remember the days without such technology. Nowadays, we are so addicted to our cell phones; we cannot imagine life without them. In the early 1990s, I remember people in Haiti who wished to send a long message or connect with their loved ones emotionally in the United States having to send a letter or recordings of their voices on a tape recorder via mail.

During this same time, there was a political shift taking place in the world. The Soviet Union had just collapsed, and the U.S. was the sole superpower in the world. Their arrogant and racist foreign policies were felt harshly by the Haitian people. On my father's end, the pressure of living in a racist country could be felt through his voice when we spoke over the phone about money and hunger in Haiti. I could tell he was also under a lot of pressure. I didn't know nor was I able to understand his struggle, but I knew his life in the U.S. was not easy, although it may have been more comfortable.

We were both experiencing pressure coming from the spirit of the colonial world. I felt that mine was more extreme. Nevertheless, they were both pressures coming from white establishments. Even until this day, I had never fully bonded emotionally with my father. We are two different men with diametrically opposed interests and aspirations. I am proud of him because he is a good father and a good son, but he is not a good husband. I think this is partly because he integrated too much into U.S. culture. The Haitian ancestors wrote on our sacred document that to be "worthy of being a Haitian man, you have to be a good father, a good son, [and] a good husband." He didn't treat my mother with respect nor the women who came into his life thereafter. We have not healed emotionally nor connected as much as I would like us to, and a big part of the reason is that I am not driven by material success as much as he would like me to be. To my father, I have not achieved anything since I moved to Miami from Haiti.

I believe another part of the reason is that he doesn't like to speak about his past or his upbringing. His pain, grief, and traumas are all suppressed, perhaps because they are too heavy or painful to deal with. I can feel his wounded spirit by the simple things that trigger him. He is a loving father but emotionally incarcerated by his experience as an immigrant, a black man, a naturalized U.S. citizen, a worker, and a son of Haiti in the United States. As an immigrant, he was not welcome like the Cubans were in Miami. As a Haitian man and a worker, he was at the bottom of the social ladder. And as a son of Haiti, he was reminded every day of how terrible it was to be Haitian in Miami in the 1990s, and how the people who looked like him were portrayed as thugs and criminals in the corporate media. This form of psychological warfare is destructive to the human spirit and overall wellness. Because of his past, he often speaks with aggression as if he would be confronted at any moment, and he embodies old-school masculinity, being hardened emotionally and out of balance with himself. He finds it hard to express love to his children and family but displays it best by being a provider. Like most Indigenous people, he is strong mentally and physically, but the fact that he is living in a world of machines causes him to remain out of balance like most men living in the West. He carries a lot of traumas and hurt from the ancestors and his personal journey. This is what I noticed by watching and listening to him when we had our first conversation in Haiti, over the phone, and then later in Miami.

I met with my father once more before moving to the U.S. when he flew to Haiti to marry a beautiful light-skinned and bougie woman in 1992 named Rachel. It appears she was his childhood sweetheart, and her husband had recently passed away. Around the same time, the United Nations, Canada, and the United States had just put a severe economic embargo on Haiti, making daily life that much more difficult. Food and gas were rationed since gas stations were not open, and food was not being imported. Due to the Dominican Republic being next door, the business was being conducted on the borders in order to survive. People managed to purchase gas in large 4ft x 2ft containers and sell it per gallon on the street so that business could continue the island.

I had a feeling that my father's new wife never loved him. She was a French-speaking light-skinned woman while my father is a very dark-skinned man who doesn't speak French. From the start of the relationship, I foresaw what Karl Marx describes as a "class struggle." The class struggle between the French-speaking and light-skinned Haitians against the full-blooded descendants of Africa. This is the same class struggle I explained at the beginning of this story between General Jean-Jacques Dessalines and General Pétion over the future of the island. This time, the struggle was interpersonally between my father and his newly beloved Rachel and with the national politics of

Haiti. Rachel described my father as a "manfoubin," someone who takes life lightly, and by the time I arrived in Miami, she had already left him brokenhearted. Before I get into more details about my father, I want to go back to my upbringing in Haiti and the events that have shaped my character and painted my world view.

The Architect of the universe cast my spirit on Haitian soil the year of 1979, an eventful and very turbulent year in the world of politics. The Western World was going through its cycle of social turmoil and upheaval for the great awakening. Some Indigenous cultures in North America had prophesied the '70s as the Year of the Seventh Fire in their calendars. The year many children would be born from the four corners of the Earth with sacred and long-forgotten instructions to rebirth Mother Earth. I am not sure if I am one of those children, but ever since I was a boy, I knew that I had a noble mission. Scripture states, "Before I formed you in the womb I knew you before you were born I set you apart; I appointed you as a prophet to the nations." When I first came across those words on my journey for wisdom, I didn't understand their meaning. It sounded to me as though humans didn't have the free will that was supposedly given after God's covenant with Noah, and God was dictating human affairs. But as I grew older and wiser, I learned that there is no accident nor coincidence in life.

There is a divine order in this universe, and there are spiritual laws that govern our planet and the cosmos. The birds, trees, oceans, the sun, the moon, and the stars are all following the natural order of the divine. Humans are the only species who are arrogant enough to believe that they can live outside of the divine laws of creation. We are the only ones who do not follow the sacred instructions of life; the only species who believe being born with a certain skin complexion and color is a badge of shame or privilege on this beautiful planet we all call home. Although this sickness first originated in Europe, the cancer has spread everywhere. The human family has been lost for a long time. Now is the time to find ourselves and discover our voices. Indigenous knowledge is what we need in order to restore natural order and beauty on the planet. The Indigenous elders were right on so many things they predicted. The children of the seventh fire are here to protect our planet. They were living in harmony with spirit, so they were able to see the end at the beginning. I am fully convinced now that I was brought into this world in the year nineteen seventy-nine by the will of God. The feelings I had as a child about our world became stronger as an adult. The fire that was burning in my heart as a boy intensified as a man. Because of this, I have concluded that my conception and birth was not by accident or just simply a one-night stand, as my father and I formerly believed. It was part of a great master plan.

Life works in such a mysterious way. We will never be able to penetrate the wisdom of the spirit or understand the thoughts of God like Albert Einstein was seeking to do. To me, this is akin to chasing the wind. He is reported saying; "I want to know God's thoughts; the rest are details." The truth is that no matter how brilliant the mind is, our intellect is limited. It may help us understand the world around us, but it will never help us understand the spirit world. We will never know God's thoughts because as humans, we are too small in the web of life. We are not even the size of a mustard seed in all of creation. God begins knowing how everything will be in the end and works back to the beginning. As humans, we start everything from the beginning without any knowledge of how things will end yet continue to move forward. This is the fundamental difference that I believe exists between European colonizers and Indigenous people. European colonizers do not understand the world of spirits and are led by greed and materialism. Indigenous people are connected with spirits and do not understand the European fascination with materialism and greed.

The year of my birth, many symbolic and momentous events took place around the globe to prepare me for my mission. All these events, including the momentous movement that gave birth to modern Hayti in 1804, are connected. In 1979, the convention on the elimination of all forms of discrimination against women was adopted by the United Nations General Assembly. The late and beloved Toni Morrison was selected to speak to the graduating class of white women at Bernard College. That same year, former Black Panther leader JoAnne Deborah Byron, popularly known as Assata Shakur, was arrested and became the first woman to be incarcerated in an all-male prison where she was subjected to many indignities including being sexually assaulted by the prison guards. On my journey from innocence to wisdom, they have both taught me a lot about U.S. society and the indignities of being black and being a woman in the United States. Assata escaped from U.S. prison to Cuba, where she has resided ever since. Toni Morison just recently transitioned to the spirit world.

Seeing all these events surrounded by my birth and the story of how I was born forces me to believe that I was born for this moment in history to defend Mother Earth and advance the sacred cause of women in Haiti and around the world. In 1979, Bill Clinton, Haiti's biggest foe since Thomas Jefferson, became governor of Arkansas following a visit to Haiti with his partner in crime, Hillary. So much more was happening in our hemisphere and around the world at the time. In the island of Grenada, there was a socialist revolution taking place, Maurice Bishop led the first black and only English speaking revolution in the Caribbean, overthrowing the U.S. backed dictator, Eric Gairy, Margaret Thatcher became the first female prime minister of England, and in the United States, a new generation of women were beginning what is now termed as the second wave of feminism to assert their social and political rights.

In Havana, Fidel Castro was on fire and ready to blow up the world in defense of the Cuban Socialist Revolution. He was one of the founding members of the non-aligned movement. In 1979, he hosted the summit right in the backyard of the United States and read the declaration of the non-aligned movement, which consisted of 125 former colonized countries. The mission of the non-aligned movement was to help former colonized countries in Africa to protect and defend their newly won "national independence, sovereignty, territorial integrity, and security." Our world was divided by two great political powers with extremely different visions - the United States and the Soviet Union. The countries involved in the non-aligned movement wanted to chart their own paths and control their own destinies, as they should.

The leaders and founding members of the non-aligned movement knew the United Nations was an umbrella of western imperialism and that their voices would have never been heard on that platform. They came together as one body to resist what they described as Neocolonialism, be it under the capitalist system or the socialist system. Haiti was not a member of the non-aligned movement because the U.S. government was supporting Jean-Claude Duvalier, who like his father, was president for life. The U.S. government helped to keep the father and son in power because corporate America didn't want another socialist revolution, like Cuba, to take place in the Americas. They did everything in their power to keep both Duvaliers in power, including turning their heads against the gross human rights violations that were occurring in Haiti during their rule. President Jean-Claude Duvalier was ousted on February 7, 1986 after he was no longer needed or useful to them. The colonial establishment sent one of their powerful agents to deliver the message.

I was seven years old at the time. I don't remember much about his regime except that there was some law and order in the country and the energy was oppressive and fearful. The Duvaliers, father and son, were governing the country with an iron fist. They were anti-communists and adopted the Machiavellian philosophy of fear and death to rule by silencing their political opponents and assassinating their rivals. His private army, the Tonton Macoutes, got away with gross and unspeakable violations against human rights. There was no freedom of speech nor freedom of the press, no organization of American states to monitor elections, and no human rights organizations like the United Nations or Amnesty International to put pressure on their regime.

Business was good for the super-rich in the United States, and the corporate media kept completely silent about the Duvalier's brand of dictatorships. For the capitalist class in the United States, profit trumps human rights and democracy in the developing world. Big business pretty much controls the U.S. democracy, and the media were very happy about the state of things in Haiti at the time. Companies like Nike and Fruit of the Loom along with multiple baseball companies and other textile manufacturers have already signed a 20-year contract with the Haitian government to legally exploit workers in Haiti as they can get away with paying zero taxes to the Haitian government. In 1814, Baron de Vastey said that the colonial system was based on white dominance, massacre or enslavement of black people. Today in 2019, I can attest that the current democracy I am experiencing in the United States is a continuation of the European colonial system. It is based on white domination and the enslavement of black and brown people in the name of mass incarceration and the impoverishment of their communities.

Haiti was like a corporate plantation, in plain words, and the white politicians didn't have a problem with it. White tourists were visiting, staying in luxurious hotels, and enjoying the rich culture and beauty of the island while repression and hunger slowly killed the Haitian people. When Duvalier and his family were ousted on February 7, 1986, I became conscious socially and politically. The ouster of Jean-Claude Duvalier shocked and awakened my spirit as a child probably almost the same way many U.S. Americans were shocked and awakened politically when Donald Trump was elected as the 45th president of the United States in November 2016. It was a defining moment in Haitian history just as much as Donald Trump's victory is right now for the U.S. because it meant that the Haitian people would either follow the path that Emperor Jean-Jacques Dessalines had paved or the path that Toussaint L'Ouverture and Pétion had paved. Very different men with very different visions for the island.

Emperor Jean-Jacques Dessalines liberated Hayti on January 1, 1804 and re-established it as a black state and Indigenous warrior nation. President Pétion, whose father was a white colonist and was educated in Paris under the French, wanted Hayti to be a republic without the institution of slavery the colonizers in the United States held onto so dearly after their War of Independence. Alexandre Pétion's vision of Hayti becoming a republic came to reality after his death and almost twenty years after Emperor Jean-Jacques Dessalines was assassinated. Dessalines believed the European colonizers were our natural enemies due to the foundation of their wealth being based on the death and oppression of black and brown people all over the planet. Pétion believed that the republic form of government was more modern and democratic than the Indigenous warrior nation under Dessalines' rule. The Duvaliers, on the other hand, wanted to govern Haiti as a republic in the spirit of Emperor Jean-Jacques Dessalines, yet Papa Doc raised up the black and red flag (the official colors of the Haytian army) and used the coat of arms that Pétion and Boyer adapted after Dessalines' assassination. Immediately, there was a major contradiction. This contradiction has caused more suffering and death in Haiti than anything else. The White House supported him in power solely because he was an anti-communist, not because they care about peace, harmony, or democracy on the island. The white establishment sees Haiti as a symbol of black power and leadership, and they know that if she thrives, the black world will thrive as well.

I began to pay close attention to Haiti's politics after Duvalier was ousted. I watched and listened more closely to every dialogue on democracy and revolution. Living less than a minute from the monument of Emperor Jean-Jacques Dessalines and five minutes from St. Jean Bosco, the parish of then father Jean-Bertrand Aristide, I spent most of my afternoons at the church observing and learning from the elders discussing the history of the Catholic church in Haiti and the legacy of Emperor Jean-Jacques Dessalines. These topics are diametrically opposed to one another.

At the same time, Father Jean-Bertrand Aristide was becoming popular. He was using the colonial platform to preach and call out U.S. racist policies and interference in Haiti's internal affairs. He was also calling out the corrupt light-skinned Haitian elite who are often more willing to collaborate and conspire with France, the Duvalier's family, and his henchmen. As Father Aristide's popularity and influence grew, the Haitian people saw him as an authentic leader. They trusted him because he seemed fearless and unapologetic. Father Aristide's parish became a center of hope, and people from all the major slums in Port-au-Prince would come to hear and see him every Sunday for mass. He was the most popular figure among marginalized people in ,La saline Cite-Soleil, Tokyo, and Pont-Rouge. Like Toussaint L'Ouverture, he was unapologetically black on a colonial platform.

The Catholic church is one of Haiti's fiercest and softest enemies. They were expelled from the land by Emperor Jean-Jacques Dessalines before the decolonization campaign began at the dawn of the new year in 1804, and they came back onto Haitian soil to recolonize the spirit of the Haitian people in 1935, right after the brutal U.S. military and political occupation ended. Taking advantage of this resurgence of the church, Father Jean-Bertrand Aristide used the Catholic platform to make a name for himself in history.

There were no opportunities for young men in Haiti, so joining the colonial institution was seen by many young intellectuals as a suitable alternative to escape poverty. One of my good friends, Raoul, who attended Father Aristide's masses regularly, asked me to join him for service the next day. I am not sure exactly why I decided against it, but whatever the reason was, it may have saved my life. That Sunday service on September 11, 1988, the Parish was targeted by political mobs, and many attendees were massacred. This came to be known as the St. Jean-Bosco Massacre. Some fifty people were killed, and more than a hundred were gravely wounded in an attempt to assassinate Father Jean-Bertrand Aristide, who was a threat to the white establishment and the corrupt light-skinned elite in Haiti at the time. That day is forever etched into my memory and spirit as the day I lost part of my innocence as a boy.

Raoul survived the massacre by following Father Aristide after he removed his robe and exited through the back of the parish. I heard about the massacre minutes after it was over. It happened early and quickly that Sunday morning. Dead bodies were everywhere, and heavy smoke was coming from the church due to it being set on fire. I was in shock and was traumatized. The parish was less than five minutes from where I lived in Pont-Rouge, and although I was glad that my friend Raoul survived, I was not the same child anymore.

The most painful part for me was learning about how even a pregnant woman was killed. Sperencia was brutally stabbed in the stomach while praying in the church. There isn't a significant difference between the St. Jean-Bosco Massacre and the Charleston Church Massacre that occurred in 2015. They were both carried out by broken and misguided young men who still believed in colonialistic ideologies. I couldn't understand the reason why people would commit such an unimaginable crime.

I was taught by an Indigenous elder who once said that God gives us two eyes - one to see the physical world and the other to see the spiritual world. After that massacre, my physical eyes became wide open. I felt in the core of my being that something was drastically wrong with humanity and the world we inhabit. I have always felt it in my spirit as a child, but that day I was convinced, and every cell in my body agreed. Another part of my innocence was lost, and a great desire to heal and connect with my ancestors was ignited.

On September 11, 1988, I took the first step on my journey to wisdom, or from boyhood to manhood. With the guidance of the ancestors, I became consciously unconscious of myself and continued to take baby steps daily on this long journey of self-discovery. The spirits were now working on their own time, aligning me with the fire of the ancestors. I began to speak and ask myself some big questions. Why would God allow evil to triumph over good? What's wrong with this world? A hunger for knowledge and thirst for righteousness was slowly developing in me. Every day since then, I have followed Haiti's politics while listening to the elders and learning the way of the ancestors.

After the attempted assassination of Father Jean-Bertrand Aristide, he became more popular among the suffering masses. Many people in Haiti began to believe that he was the rebirth of one of the Haitian heroes or that he was invincible and had supernatural powers. The Haitian people believe the U.S. government was behind the attempted assassination of Aristide, while many others believe it was the corrupt status quo in Haiti in partnership with the Catholic hierarchy.

A few months before, in an interview before the massacre, Father Aristide spoke with a foreign journalist about the social and political challenges of Haiti. He stated that "the solution is revolution, first in the spirit of the gospel; Jesus could not accept people going hungry. It is a conflict between classes, rich and poor. My role is to preach and organize." Many people believe that the statement was the reason the massacre took place. He mentioned the issue of class and wealth, which is often associated with a Marxist agenda. He was suspended and later expelled from the church for his engagement in social activism. The hierarchy accused him of inciting violence and hatred. In a public statement, Father Aristide defended himself, stating "the crime of which I stand accused is the crime of preaching food for all men and women."

I don't remember hearing about him much after that statement, only that his *Lavalas* Movement was born. means flood in Haitian Creole. His movement was attempting to cleanse the country of corruption and bad spirits, and Father Jean-Bertrand Aristide, popularly known in Haiti as "titid," became the most loved and powerful man in modern Haitian history. Soon after, he was recruited by the people to join the presidential race and won against the former World Bank official and United Nations agent, Marc Bazin, who was also the former Minister of Finance and Economy under the dictatorship of Jean-Claude Duvalier.

Bazin had a lot of money behind his campaign, and the Haitian people had only the spirits of the ancestors. On election day, the *Lavalas* Movement, in what was literally a social revolution, elected Jean-Bertrand Aristide as the next president of the Republic of Haiti. On December 16, 1990, Jean-Bertrand Aristide was elected as the president, and on February 7, 1991, he took the oath of office. The country began a new chapter in its history. This was the first time I remember seeing the people of Haiti happy. They were united as one family with one heartbeat and one mind, as my Indigenous family would say during a ceremony. The beautiful and invincible energy that first vibrated on January 1, 1804 at Gonaïves was back in Haiti. People were cleaning their community and greeting each other like brothers and sisters. The powerful and ancestral energy I felt cannot be described with words. It's unfortunate that people living in colonized territories, which in my opinion are countries that are still governed by whites, may never have this experience during their lifetime. It was heartfelt energy that was both triumphant and pure.

I learned from this experience that freedom and democracy were two different things; freedom is a powerful feeling of love and joy, while democracy is a vehicle to help us get to the experience of freedom individually and collectively. I have never experienced this feeling of freedom in the United States, even though Western politicians love to boast about it. Since coming to the U.S., I have only ever experienced freedom in one environment during a three-day ceremony called Healing Turtle Island. This event was hosted in Maine in 2016 by an Indigenous woman named Sherry Mitchell (Weh'na Ha'mú Kwasset). This feeling of freedom doesn't exist in spaces occupied mainly by European colonizers or their descendants. Furthermore, the feeling of true freedom, a balance of ego and spirit, cannot be described entirely in colonial languages due to the lack of spirit and dominance of egocentrism that exists in European culture.

The first six months of Aristide's seven-month rule, ninety percent of the population in Haiti lived harmoniously. Although nothing had changed materially for the people, it seemed as though life was good. However, like Christ says, "Man should not live on bread alone." We didn't yet have bread to eat, but we didn't care because we had each other's back. We were getting ready to heal relations and build a nation of brothers as our ancestors wanted to establish in 1804. The Haitian family was starting to come together in a good way. There was only one problem. The colonized and the light-skinned Haitian elite didn't like President Aristide from the start.

The resentment that mulattoes, or the mixed-race population, had for former slaves like Toussaint L'Ouverture and Jean-Jacques Dessalines during French colonial rule had not been healed yet. Shortly after Aristide's inauguration, the same thing that happened to Emperor Jean-Jacques Dessalines happened to Aristide. A mixed-race General by the name of Raoul Cédras, in partnership with the white establishment, overthrew him in a bloody military coup on September 29, 1991 at around two in the morning. The only difference is that Aristide wasn't murdered due to the division among the soldiers who captured him. When I woke up the next day, the country was under siege and the beautiful and loving energy we reveled in for a brief time quickly switched to fearful and hateful energy. The Haitian people knew right away that the U.S. government and France were behind the violent overthrow of the president. "Se blan yo ki bay kou sa! Dèpi ras nwa ap meté tèt ansam, blan yo toujou ak kraze and divizé nou," said one of Aristide's supporters. In English, this translates to "The whites are behind the coup. Whenever black people start getting together to heal, the white establishment always creates division and chaos among us."

People were being shot indiscriminately in and out of their homes to prevent them from taking to the streets in support of the president. Lifeless bodies were piled up in the open just like they were after the January 12, 2010 earthquake, and transported in trucks, tap-taps, and vans to Titanyen, a village known in Haiti for dumping the bodies of dead political activists.

In 1991, I was twelve years old, the same age that my mother was when she left Anse-à-Veau seeking a better future in Port-au-Prince. I was now experiencing one of the darkest moments in modern Haitian history and in my life. My mother went to Port-au-Prince at twelve years old seeking a better life. At the same age, I was contemplating a better life outside of Port-au-Prince. I was impatiently waiting for my father to tell me when I would be emigrating to the United States, and it often seemed as if there was no hope. Hunger and political repression were killing us slowly and surely. All the European countries in control of the United Nations put a severe economic blockade on Haiti. Now, yet again, the country was paralyzed; there was no gas for public transportation, and although there was food in the country, the people couldn't afford it. From 1991 to 1994, daily life in Haiti was akin to hell on earth. I feel as though my writing is not sophisticated enough yet to explain in detail the suffering the Haitian people were forced to endure. My only hope was getting out of the country. Every month I called my father to send me money for food. At times, I even went to school feeling weak from hunger. People living in developed countries do not know the real meaning of hunger; it really is a diabolical political weapon used by the colonizers to control and exercise their power. The excruciating pain of hunger was extreme, and I soon developed the habit of lying on my stomach every day after school to alleviate the pain in order to fall asleep.

Growing up in Haiti, I didn't know much about the institution of slavery nor the many aspects of the system. I knew about some of the horrors, but I didn't know how sophisticated and well-calculated this institution was and how hunger and violence were the most effective weapons used by the colonizers to control their slaves. Frederick Douglass taught me almost everything I needed to know about the different features of slavery. Reading his words gave me much more clarity on how the system was run. He wrote in his autobiography that "starvation, the bloody whip, the chain, the gag, the thumb-screw, cat-hauling, the cat-o-nine-tails, the dungeon, the blood-hound, are all in requisition to keep the slaves in the United States."

When I looked back at the history of Haiti and U.S. relations, I noticed the similarities to slavery and how the U.S. government used food and violence to destabilize the Haitian government and control the Haitian people. They conspired for more than two centuries to strangle Haiti's economy. Bill Clinton is not the first U.S. president who tried to starve the Haitian people by destroying Haiti's capacity to produce its own food. Thomas Jefferson was the U.S. president who advised Napoleon Bonaparte to starve Toussaint L'Ouverture, the black revolutionary who paved the way for our freedom and independence in 1804. When Bill Clinton became the 43rd President of the United States in 1993, this devilish strategy became one of his top priorities for foreign policy in Haiti. This is why Hillary was a fierce advocate of the military occupation of Haiti. She wrote in her book, *Hard Choices,* in 2014 that "militarization has plentiful benefits. It can facilitate corporate investments, such as 'the gold rush' that the U.S. ambassador described following the Haiti earthquake. It can keep in check nonviolent dissidents, such as hungry Haitian workers or leftist students in Mexico..."

In Bill Clinton's autobiography, *My Life,* he writes, "June was a big month for international affairs: I tightened sanctions on Haiti; [and] Hillary and I hosted a state dinner for the emperor and empress of Japan." As someone who lived in Haiti during those sanctions, I must tell you what Bill Clinton meant to say was, "I starved the Haitian people." "Tightened sanctions" meant cutting the food supply of the Haitian people, and the people who were affected the most by his sanctions were women, children, and the elderly.

When President Aristide was ousted, Bush Senior was the commander in chief of the United States, and many people in Haiti were beginning to believe that the Republican party was for the rich and that the Democratic were for the poor when really they were two wings of the same bird. Bill Clinton was portrayed to the Haitian people as a "good white man." We rarely had electricity during the coup, but the night he won the election, the corrupt light-skinned elite gave us a few hours of electricity just to watch his presidential victory. The election was broadcasted on TNH (Haiti's National Television) as a supposed victory for the poor and oppressed in the United States, including the people of Haiti. That's how I saw it, yet the popular belief among the Haitian political activists was that President Bill Clinton was not as cruel and as evil as his Republican predecessor, George W. Bush Sr., and that the people could count on him to bring President Aristide back to Haiti.

While life continued during this peaceful transfer of power between the Republican and Democratic parties in the United States, the news on the radio every day in Haiti was about another pro-democracy advocate being assassinated or disappearing. The white world did not give a damn. The only victim who got some international coverage after he was assassinated on September 11, 1993 at St. Jean-Bosco Church was Antoine Izmery. Part of the reason is that he was a wealthy Haitian businessman of Jewish and Palestinian descent. The New York Times editors were comfortable publishing his story because his story wouldn't make its white audience uncomfortable.

Those years were dark and painful chapters in Haitian history. As I am writing this story, I can feel the emotions now that I was feeling at the time of the occurrences. I can still smell the dead bodies, the fear mothers had when their sons went missing, and the voices of the people crying for justice. I can even taste the excruciatingly painful hunger again and the emotions I felt during those times. The political repression was pure savagery and a reflection of what the ancestors described during French colonial rule.

A few days before President Aristide was brought back to power, I noticed a group of white men landed at Toussaint L'Ouverture International Airport. I know now that these were the representatives of the Organization of the American States (OAS), an organization designed to specifically suppress Haitian democracy. This group of white men gave the news that President Aristide was on his way back.

When they landed in Haiti, I knew they had come with hopeful news just by watching on television. I had seen not one white face at all during the dark days.

Exactly on October 15, 1994, President Aristide was returned to the Haitian people under the leadership of President Bill Clinton, accompanied with 20,000 U.S. troops, the same number of troops Napoleon Bonaparte sent in 1802 to restore slavery on the island. This time, Bill Clinton didn't bring a completely European Army, he included some Polish and Argentinian soldiers in this new expedition. When the news broke out, the energy of the people heightened again, and hope was rekindled. However, some of the elders were very concerned about the return of President Aristide due to the words of Dessalines' secretary telling us specifically that "if we ever see one white man with a gun in Hayti, the whole country needs to unite and declare war." In this new expedition, there were hundreds and thousands of them heavily loaded with armaments. President Aristide didn't look like or seem like the same man. Before his ouster, he was a priest. Now, he was accompanied by a light-skinned Haitian American woman dressed in a fancy outfit. Many Haitian people believed he was whitewashed in Washington during his years in exile. At this point, I was getting ready to move to the United States, and I didn't care much about Haiti's politics. I was happy and excited to see the American people, but I was a little frightened at the same time because of war movies like *Platoon*. The abuses and injustices committed by the U.S. military occupation of Haiti in 1915 were still opened wounds in my heart and spirit. The crimes committed by racist white southerners in Haiti during those years of occupation were unspeakable and hard for me to process as a teenager and watching war movies like *Platoon* tainted my views of the Euro-American male.

I am still on this journey of healing from traumas and pain stemming from colonial contact so that I can see my brothers of white skin in a good way. It's not an easy journey. There are many ancestral and personal traumas that I carried from the ancestors unknowingly.

I became comfortable seeing U.S. soldiers on Haitian soil after I noticed many of my black-skinned American brothers and women in the midst. I didn't know what to expect from the soldiers because their presence looked and felt like a full-scale military invasion and the Haitian people knew it right away. The most sophisticated killing machines the U.S. government had invented at that time were on Haitian soil, and we knew this was the same old story of white people stealing resources and materials to enrich themselves. The people gave Bill Clinton the benefit of the doubt in the beginning, but now they were watching him closely.

On my end, I was interested in getting to know white people. They had always been a wonder to me, and I wanted to learn about their history and what motivated them in life. The U.S. military invasion unfolded into a military occupation in 1994, two years before I left Haiti for the United States. The soldiers were friendly in the beginning, but after securing their bases and putting fences around them, the friendliness was over. I knew something was wrong, but I was more interested in flirting with the female soldiers. For every female soldier I encountered, I used the same line to start a conversation with. "Hey, you. What's your name?" Some of them told me their names, and many of them ignored me.

The first day the U.S. armed forces landed on Haitian soil was a show of force and demonstration of white power and military technology. I was in awe of the tanks and machines of death deployed in Haiti. More than 10,000 trucks, Humvees, Apache helicopters, and military tanks loaded on the capital city of Port-au-Prince and quickly surrounded the country. As mentioned earlier, Bill Clinton made it very obvious to the Haitian people that he came to occupy the land and suppress democracy. We didn't know what was said or signed between President Bill Clinton and Aristide behind the scenes, but we felt an energy of darkness over Haiti.

The first U.S. military invasion and occupation of 1915 was composed mostly of white males from the most racist states in the South. However, Bill Clinton's invasion of Haiti was multi-racial and multi-gendered. Like Frederick Douglass predicted in his speech delivered in 1865, the snake changed its skin. The new soldiers were as diverse as the colors of the rainbow. I bonded naturally with a few of the black soldiers; Black Americans were the coolest people on the planet. They were not projected as cruel and as merciless as the white soldiers I watched in Hollywood movies, which were very popular in Haiti prior to the invasion. The way they dressed and spoke always looked cool and sounded poetic to me. Young people in Haiti, including myself, looked up to all the Black American superstars. It was as if we passed them the torch of freedom to continue upholding the light of liberty and justice for all on the American continent. I was and still am proud of them. I believe that they are the model Americans. In Haiti, our spirits were being stifled, and the economy was being crippled by the white world, so we couldn't stand tall like our Black American brothers and sisters in the United States. They were our shining stars and hope for those difficult and dark days.

I looked at the black struggle like this: Haiti upheld the dignity of black people and people of color all over the world in the nineteenth century, and in the twentieth century my Black-American brothers and sisters continued this noble responsibility. During the U.S. occupation, I recall one moment when I approached a white woman with blonde hair and blue eyes named Tanya. I was naturally attracted to her for many reasons. Firstly, I had never seen a woman that white with blue eyes in Haiti. Secondly, she was very friendly, feminine, and strong. These are some of the qualities I realized that I loved about all women as a man, but as a boy, I didn't understand. I thought I was attracted to her because her skin, hair, and facial features were different from the women I was used to in Haiti.

Tanya was stationed at a base in Pont-Rouge, right next to the monument of Emperor Jacques I, the black hero and liberator of Haiti. Every hour or two, she was replaced by another soldier who happened to always be a Black-American man or woman. I would often speak to the black male soldiers, but not the female ones because I was already interested in Tanya, the white woman. Every time she was relieved from duty for the day, I couldn't wait for sunrise the next day to come.

She taught me English, and I taught her Haitian creole. I told her that one day I would be traveling to the United States and she gave me her phone number in New York to contact when I did.

One day on my usual route to school in passing her usual station, I was heartbroken to find out that she was replaced and taken to a different military base. The person who replaced her was a proud and upright Black American man named Jerome. I asked him of her whereabouts, and he advised that she might be patrolling around in the northern part of the country at night. I was devastated. Seeing that I was saddened by the fact she was gone, he attempted to console me by saying, "She is not beautiful. You should talk to a black woman instead. There are plenty in Haiti." I was not budged, and he noticed, so he added that Tanya was ugly and that her nose was like a chicken's beak. I will never forget when he made a triangle with his thumb and index fingers for emphasis. I didn't understand why he spoke unkindly of her. I had a human connection with her and was interested in learning about her as a person. As the Indigenous elders say, "We are all related," and she is a distant relative. It wasn't until after a decade of living in the United States that I really understood the racial antagonism of his words.

I believe the United States is a racialized and racist society, and everything is seen through a racial lens. The human perspective doesn't exist yet; it's either black or white. Racial tension and antagonism are the way the ruling elite control and oppress the people and the social construct, which is a big elephant hiding in the U.S.' closet. When you are living outside of the United States, you can't see it. Hollywood paints a beautiful picture for the world, but the moment you set foot in the U.S., if you have a good sense of observation, you can see racism slowly destroying the American spirit and government.

Being born in Haiti, I thought the Haitian revolution taught the white world everything to know about black people. I imagined that the white establishment abandoned their racist ideologies and accepted all children of the Earth as members of the same human family. What I didn't know was that Haiti was an exception to the rule in the Americas. The colonial world was 200 years behind Hayti in spirit. I really believed everyone was living in a post-colonial and thus post-racial world. However, once I moved to the United States, I learned more about colonial history, including my own Haitian history, and then realized how mighty and pioneering the Haitian revolutionary heroes were. They re-established Hayti, not only as a haven for black and brown people but also as the only post-colonial nation in the Western Hemisphere at the time.

Bill Clinton officially ended the U.S. military presence in Haiti with an empty speech on March 31, 1995. With the U.S. soldiers exiting Haiti, they were quickly replaced by the United Nations' so-called "peacekeepers" from Bangladesh, one of the most impoverished countries on our planet. It seemed as though people who were oppressed were now being used to suppress another oppressed country.

I was counting down the days to start my new journey northwest to the United States, so I wanted to practice speaking English with the American soldiers every day. My goal from the beginning was to integrate into U.S. society in all aspects, so I was not pleased to see the soldiers from Bangladesh because they didn't represent democracy or hope to me. Their country wasn't doing well, so I didn't believe they could teach us anything about democracy. After all, I didn't know anything about Bangladesh except that it was an underdeveloped and impoverished country like Haiti.

My father came to Haiti at the dawn of January 1996 to bring me back to the U.S. and into the next chapter of my life. I was no longer interested in Haiti nor her politics but was instead looking forward to my new and exciting life in Miami and meeting the American people. I had experienced too much political unrest, state violence, hunger, and trauma in Haiti. Too many people were suffering, especially my mother. She was suffering too much.

Growing up in Port-Rouge, political discussions were front and center in almost every conversation among young people. I was tired of politics and wanted to enjoy peace and stability. By the age of sixteen, I saw more bloodshed and mutilated bodies than I would have liked to. I felt moving to the United States was the best thing that could have happened to me.

My mother told me not to say a word about leaving the country to anyone so that jealous people wouldn't put a spell on me. I left my neighborhood the night before and slept at one of my father's aunt's home. It was a beautiful Sunday afternoon on January 14, 1996 when my mother, uncle and younger brother took me to the airport to wish me safe travels and good luck on the next chapter of my life. I was a shy sixteen-year-old going on seventeen but full of ancestral fire. My mother was sad to see me leave, but she knew it was necessary if I would ever reach my full potential and accomplish all that my heart desired. After giving her a warm embrace, she looked me in the eyes and said, "don't forget where you come from." Then turned to my father and said, "I am giving you your son. He is now a man," to which my father didn't reply.

In my father's mind and heart, he felt he was making up for the years he was not in my life by taking me out of the misery that existed in Haiti at the time. I embraced my mother a second time, hugged my uncle and brother, and sadly walked past the iron gates to board the next flight to Miami. It was my first time on an airplane. I was experiencing mixed emotions. I was saddened to leave my homeland, family, and friends but excited to meet new people and make new friends. I was even more excited to start the journey I had always dreamed of. The sadness of leaving my beloved family and friends behind almost became too much to bear when I landed in Miami. I didn't know when I was going to see them again.

Chapter 2

United States of America

UNITED STATES DECLARATION OF INDEPENDENCE
JULY 4, 1776

"When in the course of human events, it becomes necessary for one people to dissolve the political bands which have connected them with another, and to assume among the Powers of the earth, the separate and equal station to which the laws of nature and nature's God entitle them, a decent respect for the opinions of mankind requires that they should declare the causes which impel them to the separation. We hold these truths to be self-evident, that all men are created equal, that they are endowed by their Creator with certain unalienable rights; that among these are life, liberty, and the pursuit of happiness; that to secure these rights, governments are instituted among men, deriving their just powers from the consent of the governed; that whenever any form of government becomes destructive of these ends it is the right of the people to alter or abolish it, and to institute a new government laying its foundation on such principles, and organizing its powers in such form as to them shall seem most likely to affect their safety and happiness. Prudence, indeed, will dictate that governments long established should not be changed for light and transient causes; and accordingly, all experience had shown, that mankind are more disposed to suffer, while evils are sufferable than to right themselves by abolishing the forms to which they are accustomed. But when a long train of abuses and usurpations, pursuing invariably the same object, evinces a design to reduce them under absolute despotism, it is their duty to throw off such government, and to provide new guards for their future security."

Welcome to Miami

"I have a dream that one day this nation will rise up and live out the true meaning of its creed: "We hold these truths to be self-evident: that all men are created equal." - Martin Luther King, American patriot and founding father, (August 28th, 1963)

"We are confronted primarily with a moral issue. It is as old as the Scriptures and is as clear as the American Constitution. The heart of the question is whether all Americans are to be afforded equal rights and equal opportunities" - John F Kennedy, 35th president of the United States (June 11th, 1963)

I arrived at Miami International Airport on the evening of Sunday, January 14, 1996. I don't remember the exact time, but I am almost certain it was around six or seven p.m. I sat by the window on the flight, so the beautiful scenery of Downtown Miami was the first thing I was mesmerized by upon landing. For a short period of time, it felt like I was on a different planet. The skyscraper buildings were lit. They looked like architectural Christmas trees of the city. I was in awe of their beauty and height. Most of the images of I had of Miami came from watching Miami Vice. Miami Beach was the only image I had of the city. Stepping out of the airport, it felt like I was just beginning my first scene in a new Miami Vice series. I was excited and ready for the adventure. I was most excited about the beautiful women and the beach I used to see in the hit TV series.

As my father and I were driven out of the airport, one of the first things I remember saying to myself was, "I hope my father lives in a white neighborhood." I said that because I felt in my spirit that part of the reason I came to the United States was to learn how to be successful from white American people. I wanted to learn from them and share the history of Haiti with them. I was also eager to learn about U.S. society and U.S. history in order to gain knowledge and wisdom so that I could one day go back home and empower the Haitian people economically. I thought white people in the United States had developed a science of wealth creation. The 1990s had a huge effect on U.S. capitalism. America was a symbol of economic success and prosperity for almost all outsiders looking in.

In my young mind, I thought the United States had developed a secret knowledge they didn't want to share with the developing world. The developing world was behind economically and impoverished because they didn't know about this new science of wealth creation. In colonial history, I was taught that the science of wealth creation was based on the enslavement of black people and the genocide of the native people. I thought the United States was post-colonial. I was eager and hungry to learn how white people created their wealth. Countries like the United States and Canada had always been projected as rich and successful modern nations. The people I saw on television, who happened to be mostly white, seemed happy and prosperous. I had never seen a poor white person on television. They were either affluent or living in the middle class. The only time I saw poverty in an American movie was in the classic comedy, *Coming to America.* Eddie Murphy, who played the African prince, gave a bag full of money to two white homeless men who were sleeping in the freezing cold in New York. That was my first and only time seeing poor whites in a movie.

I left behind so much poverty in my community and my family, so I felt a strong desire in my spirit to be successful and had a very powerful urge to make a difference. I didn't know what success would look like to me because as a son of Haiti, I didn't and still do not think and speak of success in the same way Americans do. I didn't and still do not see success as purely an individual achievement like white people do. From the day I was born, the first thing I remember hearing was, "Your ancestors are your role models." They were the most successful men in modern history; they led the first and only successful slave revolt in human history. The success of the revolution rebirthed Hayti and shifted the planet. It was a triumph for the human race. The human race had advanced forward because of the Haitian ancestors. So I grew up believing that being successful is supposed to be more about collective wellness than one person or group. When a musician composes a beautiful melody, he or she enjoys it. But it's for the collective culture of the human family. As a son of Haiti, I know there will be some people who will always benefit more from the success of any endeavor than others because of sacrifices rendered. However, if the whole is not well, neither are the parts. Making a difference to me was a civic duty and a moral obligation.

This is what I was taught in my community growing up, and this what I learned from my elders and ancestors. I arrived at my new home in Miami Gardens at around 8:00 p.m. I felt a great sense of joy and equanimity. I had my own room for the first time, electricity twenty-four hours a day, food security and running water in the kitchen and bathroom. In less than two hours, I went from one extreme to another. I felt like I was now living a good and successful life, even though my father was not making much money working as a custodian in the Miami-Dade school system. Coming straight out of Hayti, my definition of the good life was very simple: clean water, food security, a loving home, and a safe community. I had all of the above from the first day. The only thing I was missing now was a school and a library. I didn't want to be locked up in the house. The next thing I was thinking about doing after I was settled in was finding the basketball ball court, the schools, and the public library.

I was a boy in the process of consciously becoming a man. I was full of excitement and energy. I was in my own adventure, very determined to learn and understand the way of these new people who looked and spoke differently from me. I also knew the country was young, arrogant, powerful, and offered me a lot more opportunity than my native country, so I wanted to take advantage of all of it. I wasn't afraid of working hard. I wanted to succeed so I could live the Miami lifestyle I saw on television from Haiti. Miami Vice did paint a beautiful picture of Miami for me. I really believed *Miami Vice* reflected the city of Miami. Black people who were a minority of the country were living a good life. The main characters in the TV series was a black and white man. The Spanish people were just the extras. I thought the drama series was a representation of U.S. culture and society. It would actually take me more than a decade to realize Spanish speaking people run Miami. Black and white people were the extras in the real-life *Miami Vice*.

I was yearning to integrate into American society and culture. This desire derived from my hunger to learn, succeed, and be of service. When my younger sister, who was full of love, ran up to me to say hello in a terrible and broken Haitian creole, I told her that I understood English and that she could speak to me in English. I was full of ancestral fire and ready to assimilate in U.S. culture. I am not sure what Aristide was going to do, but I wanted to be part of the American story and engage in the democratic system. I wanted to be an American. I didn't know what that meant, but what I did know was there was a lot of potential in this country. There was room for growth. At first, I hesitated about renouncing my Haitian citizenship because I was too proud of being Haitian. After a short distance in my journey, I realized it was in the best interest of Haiti to become a naturalized U.S. citizen. Before I came to Miami, I was advised by my father's ex-wife, Rachel, to watch a lot of television to pick up on American English quicker. So, the very next day, which was Dr. King's birthday, I was glued in front of the television watching TV shows and sitcoms to learn the way and culture of the "American people." The TV shows were qualitative back then.

There was no 24-hour sensational news cycle, cell phones, and other distractions, such as the internet and social media. The television was my first American classroom. There was less noise in the corporate media, and the airwaves were cleaner and healthier for a newcomer like me. I spent hours watching shows like *The Fresh Prince Bel-Air, Family Matters, The Cosby Show, Martin, Full House, Roseanne, Sister Sister, Moesha, and Friends*. I noticed the story and humor from the shows were different from actual life in America. Pains were turned into comedy for my black American brothers and sisters. The black shows were funny, but behind the humor was always a hidden statement about police harassment, racial discrimination and racial profiling of young black men. The white shows were about living the good life.

Each sitcom taught me something different about the American experience. *Full House* was about the reality of being white in the middle class in America. *Roseanne* was about the reality of being poor and white. *Friends* was about "upper-class whiteness." There weren't any main black characters in none of these shows. Black or native people were literally absent.

On the black show, *The Fresh Prince of Bel-Air*, there were many white guests and actors. The story was about a troubled and misguided young black man who went to live with his affluent black family in a predominantly white and wealthy neighborhood. So, they exhibited more of a white representation than shows like *Martin*, *Moesha*, the *Wayans Bros*. My true education about America's society and culture started by watching the comedy shows, both old and new.

A week or two after being in Miami, I went to a clinic in Miami Beach to get vaccinated so I could continue my high school education. While I was going there with my father, I realized black and white people didn't live in the same area. I could see the difference not just by the sheer number of white people across the bridge but by the difference in houses and structures of the communities. The schools, parks, and recreation centers looked a lot better than where I was living. It was very obvious for someone like me whose eyes were not yet trained to see this brutal inequality. The legacy of Jim Crow segregation (as I came to learn later) was very vivid and plain. It was a self-evident truth that the grass was greener on the white side of the fences. It actually took me more than a decade as a Miami resident to fully learn and understand what legal racism (aka Jim Crow segregation) was really about.

In Indigenous culture and language, there is no word for segregation or apartheid. Those words were foreign to my mind and spirit. I couldn't grasp the full meaning and spirit of those words. The more I got to know the challenges of my Black American brothers and sisters, the more I realized the system invented those words and systems to dehumanize and oppress them. Many of African-American family remember the signs that once prohibited them from using the public facilities whites used. They told me the house of the first black family who moved into a white neighborhood in Miami was bombed. This dark and ugly history of Miami still thrives in the local politics and is institutionalized in the private sector.

Miami is one of the most unequaled cities in the US, second worst in regard to poverty level and probably more segregated than it was in the sixties. The black population is affected severely by this man-made poverty. They are the most marginalized and the most demonized in the media. I first realized it for myself when I first visited Overtown, which was called the "colored town," when racism was legal in the '50s and '60s.

My first ten years in Miami was about trying to assimilate to the U.S. American culture. The rest was about self-discovery and awareness. I was discovering myself, finding my voice, and reconnecting with my ancestors on Turtle Island (North America). After I was done with the first immunization shots on January 22, 1996 and received my transcript from secondary school in Haiti, I was now ready and excited to begin my first day of schooling in the United States. It was something I had dreamt of as a boy in Haiti for years.

There is one American school in Haiti called Union School. It was established in 1919, two years after the brutal U.S. Marines' invasion and occupation of the island. It catered to mostly the light-skinned and affluent Haitian families. Many young people, including myself, used to dream of attending that school to learn American English. There was no way someone like me would have been able to attend because the yearly costs for attending was $15,000 U.S. dollars from ninth to twelfth grade. In the United States, I was granted the same opportunity to get an American education for free. Most of what I knew about American schools came from watching television sitcoms when I was in Haiti. I have always loved America. There was something about the U.S. Democratic experiment that I deeply admired. I wasn't sure what it was, but I was now on a journey to find out for myself what it was that I like about America and what it really means to be an American.

Enrolling in the school system was the first and most important step of that journey. I was only sixteen years old and would be turning seventeen in April. I didn't fully know what it meant to be Haitian or the son of the world's first and only self-made Black Republic. But I felt in the core of my being that it was a big responsibility, a responsibility to continue the noble legacy of my ancestors who have been demonized by the European colonizers for more than two centuries.

The only thing that mattered to me at the time was becoming a person of value and success. I had just escaped from an impoverished community and country. Being productive and successful were my most important priorities. I wanted to help my family and my native land. Did I know what it meant to be successful? I didn't! However, I was determined to learn the language and culture. I came to Miami with only one pair of red jeans and a white T-shirt. I left all of my clothes for my brothers in Haiti because I knew I was coming to a materially rich nation to make something of my life. I never doubted myself nor limited my aspirations. One of the first things a member of my family told me that was, "If you get arrested in this country, you will never get a good job. You will never be able to work for the government." And the second thing I remember learning was, "If you aren't born in the United States, you can never become a president of the American republic. You can become governor of a state, but not the president of the United States." When I heard that, I thought to myself, *Well, I am going to work in a way so that my children can become president of the United States then.*

My father didn't take me shopping for clothes for my first day of schooling. Instead, he went to his closet and gave me some of his most outdated clothes. I couldn't believe he still had them in his possessions. It was clothing that even people in Haiti wouldn't wear. I was shocked at how outdated my father was in style and in culture. Most of my father's clothes were in style in the '60s and '70s. Since it was my first day of school, and I had only been in Miami a couple of weeks, I didn't want to protest or express any spirit of ingratitude. I took the clothes from him nicely, but internally, I was pissed and angry that my father could be so outdated. I couldn't believe I was now in the United States wearing clothes that I wouldn't even wear in Haiti. It was embarrassing on my first day of school to wear that pair of green and brown disco style pants and shirt.

This was my first informal introduction of getting to know my father's style and taste. I spent almost all of my teenage years with my mother. The next chapter would be about getting to know my father, who is a very stoic and unexpressive man. My father is the epitome of old school masculinity. He lives a life of quiet dignity and independence. He has a few people he is acquainted with. He has no close friends.

I attended Miami Norland Senior High School, located five blocks from where I lived. On the first day, I went to the principal's office to get my schedule for class. I was thrilled by the experience but extremely shy. Everyone was dressed in expensive clothes, wore nice shoes, and looked very cool. The first thing I quickly noticed was the social and racial make-up of the student body. Almost all of the students were black. There were a few Spanish students sprinkled here and there, but there was not one white student. The only whites in the school were only the teachers. I was very uncomfortable because I didn't dress, speak, or act like anyone in this new environment which I was now a member of. Although they were all mostly black students, everyone looked weird to me. I didn't fully understand the language, but I was determined to learn it in a short period of time.

My homeroom class was an ESOL class, which stands for English as a Second language. I spent two hours in the ESOL class before going to lunch. After lunch, I went to a French class, which was like my second homeroom, and then proceeded to Physical Ed. Since I wanted to get a car, I took a Drivers Ed class in the summer.

The teacher of my ESOL class was a white woman named Ms. Mona. She was the kindest and most loving teacher I had throughout my duration at Norland. In that class, there were only students from Haiti and Spanish-speaking countries like Cuba, Venezuela, and Columbia. I didn't feel like I was in an American school yet because every student was born outside of the United States.

I was eager to get out of my ESOL class to learn the same thing the " real Americans" were learning. In less than three months, my dream came true. I left the ESOL class and started to take Advanced English. This small success made me feel good about myself. This success story laid the foundation for all my other successes in the school. Every day after class from that day onward, I went to the library to pick up books to take home to improve my communication skills. I loved the library and the books I had access to. To me, they were the real treasures of American society. I regarded the libraries as the greatest and the most democratic institutions in the United States. The United States was great because of the libraries. Because of this, one of the first ideas I had during my stay in the United States was to build libraries around the country." As the late Toni Morison said, "Education is itself democracy."

One of the first things I observed, aside from the fact that there were no white students in my high school, was that the students weren't as excited about learning as I was. Every day after school, almost all the students left their books in their lockers. It was the coolest thing to do. This was probably my first cultural shock. In Haiti, in order to be cool or get a girlfriend, you have to be an intellectual. You must have a natural love for learning and be able to defend yourself both ideologically and physically. I learned education was one of the weapons my ancestors used to defeat the European colonizers in their own game. The lyrics of the Haitian National Anthem remind us every day how critical education is in the fight against slavery and colonization. The culture was the opposite in the United States of America. The coolest people were the athletes, the football players, basketball players, the tough guys, and the students who word brand name shoes and clothes, such as Tommy Hilfiger, Jordan, and Polo Ralph Lauren. Those guys were the most respected. The cheerleaders loved them, and the nerds fear them. Nerds and Haitians were almost synonymous and the least respected.

Many of the Haitians born in the United States didn't want people to know they were of Haitian descent. I was confused. I didn't understand why they were so ashamed of being Haitian. When I told them Haiti is the first and only self-made Black Republic in the world, they couldn't understand what I meant. During Black History Month, while they were celebrating black American heroes and patriots like Frederick Douglass, Dr. Martin Luther King, Jr., Rosa Parks, and Malcolm X, I often asked some of my classmates if they ever heard of Toussaint L'ouverture and Jean-Jacques Dessalines. They looked at me like I was crazy and started to laugh. That was kind of my first hint that the government school system was designed, as Malcolm X said, "to miseducate black people." I was becoming more fluent in American English, so I became more interested in learning the history of the United States and the other Americas.

I moved to Miami on the eve of Dr. Martin Luther King, Jr.'s birthday. So I started to get a flashback of his voice. I remember watching a clip of him on PBS saying, "Free at last. Thank God almighty. We are free at last." King's words were shortly followed by President Kennedy's famous quote: "Ask not what your country can do for you. Ask what you can do for your country." I was captivated by Dr King's fire and personal power. My ancestral fire was lit and kindled from his. Growing up in Pont-Rouge, I heard the story of Malcolm X passingly, but I had never heard of Dr King. I said to myself, "Why was he saying, 'free at last'? Weren't black people free in the United States before?" I really didn't understand what was going on. I was confused and lost. The fiery voice of Dr King and the mellow words of President Kennedy were etched in my memory from that day onward. As a native of Haiti, who was born in the ashes of my ancestors, it was impossible to ignore King's voice and fire. He was shining too bright. We were connected ever since. The words of President Kennedy were simple and yet very profound to me as well. I grew up listening to the elders and community leaders blaming Haiti's biggest challenges on leadership. President Kennedy's quote made me feel like I was an important member of society, and that I had a role to play in making my community and nations better.

As I continued walking on my journey, his words marinated in my mind, and his words became louder in my head. After the first or second week of schooling at Miami Norland Senior High, I was taken to the library and introduced to a Haitian-American man who was in charge of it. I was proud to see a Haitian in that position. I viewed being the librarian as the most prominent position in the school after the principal.

I have always loved books and libraries. In Haiti, I didn't have access to a library because the colonizers were trying to erase our memory. Haiti's most important books and documents are hidden in European or colonial institutions. My love for books came naturally because I was always a student of life. As a child and student in Haiti, I was always excited about the first day of school. I knew my mother was going to have new books and uniforms. My first book as a child was "ti malice," meaning "little malicious." Although I find that book destructive for children, I loved it as a child because I have a natural love for printed words and images.

As I was searching for English books with French translation to improve my reading skills in my school library, I came across two books that ignited my desire to learn about systems of racial oppression. The first one was titled *Young People Speaks*. It's about children who survived the Jewish Holocaust in Hungary. The photographs of innocent and beautiful children on the cover caught my attention. The second one is *The Eyes on the Prize: Civil Rights Reader: Documents, Speeches, and Firsthand Accounts of the Black Freedom Struggle*. It is a collection of speeches and letters written by Dr. King when he was in jail. I took them both home to read, and I couldn't let them down. I was moved by the stories.

Some of the stories of the Jewish children in *Young People Speaks* reminded me of my experience in Haiti. I was able to relate to the severe hunger they went thru while hiding in the bunkers during the war. How they described the concentration camps and the occupation of Hungary by the German troops wasn't much different from the U.S. military occupation I saw prior to my arrival in the United States.

The words of Dr. King, coupled with voices of the children who survived the unspeakable horror, sparked the flame of my ancestors. I was fired up now. I wanted to know more about the roots and history of anti-Semitism and anti-black racism. I couldn't understand why the Jewish people who were literally white were being persecuted like that. It was then that I took the opportunity to read everything I could find about the Jewish Holocaust and the African American Holocaust, if I may describe the plight of my Black American brothers as such. I began connecting all the dots now and seeing Haiti from a different lens. My spirit was traveling in the past, present, and future. I couldn't believe the power structure in Europe allowed this great evil to happen. The more I learned about the Jewish Holocaust, the more I felt this should have never happened, and the more I started to see Haiti as the "modern Israel" and the United States as the "new Rome."

I had no one to ask questions about the Jewish Holocaust. Some of the Jewish people I've met were so wounded from the tragedy, they didn't want to talk about it. My eyes have been open ever since to political extremism, and the Jewish people have been in my heart and prayers as I continue walking on this journey of self-discovery.

Throughout my four years of formal learning in the public school system, I didn't learn anything about American history. The only thing I can honestly say I learned was that the U.S. school system is governed like U.S. society. It's highly segregated and racist. It's designed that way to cripple and colonized the minds of black students and leaders. As a student, I tried very hard to assimilate to the sickness of U.S. culture. I am glad it didn't work out. As I reflect, I know a huge part of my not being able to adjust is attributed to the fact that my spirit was already too indigenized. I was already molded on Haitian soil as a warrior. If I had moved to Miami at a younger age, I believe I would have been lost in U.S. society. I would have become a black version of white society.

The majority of the teachers I had in school were white, and most of them did not really know anything about the black experience. They were teaching from a colonial perspective. I was in disbelief at how arrogant and racist one of my white teachers was. It seemed to me that the established power had racial quotas for the public-school system. The number of black, white, and yellow teachers were carefully selected for schools in the black community.

One day, I remember an old white man, who looked like he was either from Texas or Mississippi, was a substitute teacher for one of my classes. He didn't seem like he was qualified for the job. He walked in the classroom with a spirit of arrogance and superiority, acting like the classroom was a colonial plantation, and we were his subjects. What shocked and vexed me the most was how frequently he used foul and abusive language towards the students. Most of the male students thought he was a gangster and were amused by the insults. I was new in the country. I didn't know the history of the word *nigger* at the time in the United States. So I thought it was culturally acceptable for anyone to use it, including this old racist white man in the classroom. He used the N-word so frequently that at one point, I started to use it as well. It wasn't until I started to dig deep in U.S. history that I understood the dark history of this word and the spirit behind why white people were using it against black people on this continent.

That day was an introductory class on the nature of the abusive relationship between blacks and whites in the United States. And I also realized that the education system was broken. There was a problem recruiting and paying teachers what they deserve. There were a lot of substitute teachers in some of my classes. For my math class, I had a Cuban teacher, who I am pretty sure now got the job mostly because he was Cuban. His Spanish accent was so thick, it was painful for the student to listen to him.

The school that I attended was not teaching me anything about history. Although I was in a predominantly black school, everything I learned about the black experience in the United States was from my own research and desire to know about my brothers and sisters in the United States. The colonial founders of the United States never intended or envisioned for black people to be freed. And they knew only education could truly liberate people. During colonial slavery, they made it illegal for enslaved people to learn how to read or write. If a black person was caught with a book, it would have been a death sentence for him or her. They knew as Frederick Douglass noted, "knowledge makes a man unfit to be a slave."

In the public school system, they create an environment where students are not very interested in reading and learning about their history. A good education was never a birthright for all American children. Working-class people, black, white, and yellow, had to fight for universal education in the United States. One of the pioneer organizers of this fight was Mary Harris Jones, popularly known as Mother Jones. She was an Irish American woman and former schoolteacher who led thousands of children in marches to protest against child labor across the country. To get the attention of the nation, she marched with them from New Jersey to New York and down to Oyster Bay to meet with President Theodore Roosevelt, so he could see the faces of children working sixty hours a week in textile mills and coal mines for the U.S.

economy. These children often carried banners and signs that said: " WE WANT TO PLAY. WE WANT TO GO SCHOOL! 55 HOURS OR NOTHING."

Many people in the United States are "woke" now. They want to blame Donald Trump for most of the sickness of the country without realizing that Donald Trump is simply exposing the European ugliness and sickness for us to heal from it. This colonial spirit and arrogance were brought over here 500 hundred years ago. The U.S. school system is and has been broken for a very long time. Just like Catholics will never look out for the interest of protestants, the people who identify themselves as white instead of American on this continent will never petition for the wellbeing and interest of black or Indigenous people of America because their ancestors built a system based on white supremacy. They enjoyed the privilege of being white more than being American.

The white establishment does not want black students to become lawyers, scientists, doctors, innovators, scholars, pioneers, and business or community leaders. They want to control the social destiny of black and brown people in this country. They are comfortable with them being athletes, hustlers, pimps, and rappers. They don't believe in freedom and democracy. At least, the white people who are in control of the major institutions of this country don't. Those institutions really aren't American institutions. They are all colonial institutions. They were established to protect and preserve whiteness. So to achieve their goal, they make sure their government invests more in the military than the education of black and brown children. America has been in a racist society from inception. Individuals like Betsy Devos and Donald Trump are just an ugly symptom and mirror of a deeply wounded and broken people and society.

From my experience and observation, the U.S. government and school system have been broken since I moved here in 1996. When I first stepped in the hallways of school and into the classrooms, it didn't even take me three months to realize something was deeply wrong with U.S. society. It was clear that the HSCT (High School Competency Test) I was forced to take in order to receive my diploma was carefully crafted by racists to keep black and brown students from progressing academically.

By the time I graduated, we had a black principal who ran the school like a prison. The teachers were afraid of him, and because he was a former football player, he let the athletes do whatever they wanted to do. One day, we were so tired of his bullshit. I helped organize a peaceful walk-out which made national news. I was quoted in the national paper the next day. Some of my teachers told me the story reached politicians in Washington and that they liked my opinion on the walk-out. Afterward, the bullying ended, and the learning environment went back to normal. I got my first social justice victory from that experience, and I became more confident and certain ever since then that I was born to make a difference.

I graduated from high school on June 16, 1999. I didn't really learn much except the lesson of kindness and beauty from my ESOL teacher, Ms. Mona and the two books I borrowed from the library about the Jewish Holocaust and the Black American Freedom Struggle. I later realized that while I was in school, I was getting most of my education from television by watching the local news and talk shows hosts, such as Oprah Winfrey and Jerry Springer. They were two different people exposing two different realities of America. Oprah used her platform to empower mostly middle-class white Americans. Jerry Springer used his to entertain and expose the brokenness of mostly poor and white Americans. I was learning a lot from those shows and the corporate media, which had a monopoly on how news and information were circulated to the people.

One of the biggest news stories I remember following in was about the O.J. Simpson trial. The country was divided along a racial line, and I didn't understand why. I noticed black people were happy that O.J. Simpson was found not guilty. However, the white population didn't see it that way. They were angry and feeling that O.J. had got away with murder. I couldn't understand what was going on because I was watching the story through post-colonial lenses. To me, the trial was about a man who allegedly killed his wife. To colonial America, the trial was about a black man who murdered a white woman. For two decades, I watched the story unfold like a reality TV show. The O.J. trial made me realize that the Haitian heroes were right about white colonizers. They are very fascinated with stories of sex, violence, and wealth.

As the story of O.J. continued to dominate mainstream media, the shocking death of Tupac Shakur made headlines, and nationally, young black men were getting shot like they were at war with each other. I was not yet able to connect the violence in the political culture of Haiti to the violence in the streets of U.S. ghettos. I learned to appreciate Tupac as an artist because he was young, black, and unapologetic. Although he was misguided, like many of my black brothers born in a racist society, he intended to be and do good. He was striving to become a good and upright man. I was shocked by his death. His music was energetically empowering to my younger self. It was hard to deal with his death because he was a huge cultural icon and a leader for young people like myself, who didn't have the language yet to express my thoughts and feelings.

I began to observe a pattern of violence, murder, and sexual assaults in mainstream media and culture. Not long after the media was saturated with the O.J. trials and Tupac and Biggie murders, a six-year-old beauty princess named JonBenét Ramsey was raped and murdered by a monstrous white man. I thought to myself, *What kind of culture is this?* I was shocked not just by the way she was murdered, but also by the motivation of her parents to enroll her in a beauty pageant at such a tender age. Almost every year after that, a sex scandal, massacre, terrorist attack, gang violence incident, or a school shooting was recycled as symptoms of a deeply wounded people and society.

Former President Bill Clinton, who in my opinion embodies and normalizes the European sickness more than any other U.S. president in my lifetime, was re-elected in 1997. Instead of using the power vested in him to lead the country in the direction of healing and transformation, he was coercing his intern Monica Lewinsky for sexual favors. The highlight of the national news was about his impeachment instead of going to the root of the problem, which I found disrespectful and undignified to the U.S. people.

While I was trying to understand what type of white man Bill Clinton was, there was another news story about death and violence. This time it was a massacre that took place at Columbine High School. Two white males walked into the school and murdered students indiscriminately. The movie *Matrix*, which came out a month before the massacre, and the music of Marilyn Manson were blamed for inspiring this senseless act of violence. I now realized that there were two Americas – one black and one white.

The white press rationalizes the death of black and brown men in the streets as part of cultural norms. They portray black people as if blackness is associated with violence and crimes. They are always in a hurry to label young and misguided black men as thugs, but then suggest that young and misguided white men are mentally ill.

I was listening to two different perspectives coming from two different types of people. Both felt a sense of entitlement to the country. Both blacks and whites are lost and deeply wounded by colonialism and slavery. They are both strangers living exiled on stolen land. They never have taken the time to listen to each other or the Indigenous people who inhabited North America thousands of years prior to their voluntary and involuntary arrivals. I saw pain, traumas, and sickness on both sides. Black Americans and white Americans are in pain.

As a son of Hayti, I was taught early to honor the Taïnos and Arawak Indians as my heroes also. They were the first Haytians and the first to resist the European colonizers. As a matter of historical fact, the liberator of Hayti, Emperor Jean-Jacques Dessalines, renamed the island Hayti in honor of the Indigenous people of the land after defeating the European army. I grew up with a spirit of gratitude, awareness, and respect for the first inhabitants of every modern nation in the Americas. I know their blood, bones, sweat, tears, and prayers are cemented in the soil. I contemplated about what their lives must have been like prior to the arrival and disruption of their way of life by the European colonizers. Sometimes, I think about their lives and how they must have felt when they were being invaded and decimated. The fear and courage they exhibited to resist the colonizers. To be oppressed on your own is extremely painful. My spirit was always yearning to connect with them and learn from them. My ancestors knew the Indigenous people had the wisdom that could help us become a better version of ourselves. That's why the Haytian warrior wanted us to walk on only the black and the red road.

After graduating from high school, I was contemplating what to do with my life. I knew I wanted to serve the Haitian community, but I didn't know how and what to do. Every other week or month, there was always a boat full of Haitian people fleeing the poverty and political unrest in the island. They were always humiliated and treated without the dignity and the respect they deserve. Former President Bill Clinton's policies were the cruelest toward the Haitian people, both in Haiti and when they landed on U.S. soil as political refugees. One Haitian refugee wrote in a letter to his family while he was in jail during Clinton's administration, " I have lost hope in the struggle for life... There is nothing left for me. Take care of my children, so they have strength to continue my struggle... I have lost hope. I am alone in my distress..."

Bill Clinton enacted the policy that became known as "wet foot, dry foot policy," which is popularly known in Little Haiti as the black foot, white foot policy. Bill Clinton crafted it specifically for Cuban immigrants who make it to U.S. shores (dry foot). They were the only ones allowed to stay in the United States if they were caught on U.S. soil. They were qualified for permanent residency right away. But if the Haitian people who were fleeing poverty and political suppression made it to shores of the United States, they were sent back. The racist logic is in Haiti, there is a democracy. In Cuba, there is a brutal dictator named Fidel Castro. For a while, I watched this unfair, unjust, and racist narrative played out over and over in corporate media.

I became more concerned about the treatment of Haitians fleeing persecution after the Elian Gonzalez custody battle. He was miraculously found by two fishermen lying in an inner tube floating at sea three miles from the coast of South Florida. His mother had drowned not too far from where he was rescued by the U.S. Coast Guard. He was treated like a European prince. He was pampered with gifts and attention from people all over the world.

After the U.S. government was attacked by religious extremists on September 11, 2001, a war on "terror" was declared. That day reminded me about the Saint-Jean Bosco massacre that occurred in Haiti on September 11, 1988, which sparked my curiosity as a boy to listen and learn about Haitian politics from my elders. September 11, 2001 did the same thing to me as a man in the United States. I began to pay closer attention to U.S. politics and listen to my Black American brothers' perspective. Before the attack , I was trying to find myself in order to achieve the "American Dream." After the attack, I didn't have the same motivation anymore. I wasn't interested in the "American Dream" anymore. I wanted to understand the "American Dream." I was so shocked and traumatized, seeing the second plane hit the World Trade Center. The trauma I experienced in Haiti as a boy on the exact same date was resurfacing. It was suppressed and never healed. I reached out to a good friend whose opinions I valued and respected. He told me the attack was a declaration of war. It was a retaliation for the pain the U.S. government inflicted around the world. That's why those extremists targeted the World Trade Center, the Pentagon, and the White House. Those institutions are symbols of oppression for black and brown people on our planet. He differentiated between an act of terrorism and an act of war. He said an act of terrorism is an attack on public places like parks, churches, and buses. An act of war is an attack on government buildings. I put some thought into what he said and let it marinated in my mind.

Meanwhile, I paid attention to U.S. domestic politics. I was listening to everyone and anyone whose perspective was different from mine. I wanted clarity. I felt the world was too chaotic and didn't make much sense. I was yearning for intellectual clarity and peace of mind. I noticed the social and political climate change. The American people were ready to attack any country. The next day, the corporate media was now reporting about anthrax being sent to people's homes, news offices, hospitals, and government buildings. According to George W Bush's book, *Decision Points*, one of the letters containing anthrax read:

> 09-11-01
>
> YOU CAN NOT STOP US.
>
> WE HAVE THIS ANTHRAX.
>
> YOU DIE NOW.
>
> ARE YOU AFRAID?
>
> DEATH TO AMERICA.
>
> DEATH TO ISRAEL.
>
> ALLAH IS GREAT.

The Bush administration invented a metric to measure the level of fears in order to rally the people behind his agenda. The invented threat ranged between yellow, red, and green. A year after the attack, on Thursday, September 12, 2002, President Bush went in front of the UN Assembly to give his reasons as to why Iraq, the third-largest oil reserve in the world was responsible for the attack on September 11, 2001. President Bush said, "In 1991, the UN Security Council through Resolution 687 demanded that Iraq renounce all involvement with terrorism and permit no terrorist organizations to operate in Iraq. Iraq's regime agreed. It broke its promise. From 1991 to 1995, the Iraqi regime said it had no biological weapons. After a senior official in its weapons program defected and exposed this lie, the regime admitted to producing tens of thousands of liters of anthrax and other deadly biological agents for use with Scud warheads, aerial bombs, and aircraft spray tanks. And that the regime continues to shelter and support terrorist organizations that direct violence against Iran, Israel and Western governments."

The UN inspectors went to Iraq but couldn't find any weapons of mass destructions that the Bush administration claimed existed. Bush rushed to war without the approval of the United Nations and exposed the real spirit of that organization's body. I was convinced then that the UN was a mutation of the League of Nations, an arm of colonialism and imperialism and a deceptive and irrelevant institution in the cause of peace around the world.

Millions marched against the war in Iraq. Neither the United Nations nor the people had the power to prevent it. As much as I was trying to achieve the American Dream, I was also becoming a man. I have learned in this capitalist system that war of plunder is a business model and very profitable. Based on the history of U.S. military intervention in other countries, I realized the people marching against the war wouldn't be able to stop it. To prevent future wars, a grassroots movement of peace had to be built. I learned that the white establishment planned its wars ahead of time. It's very possible the invasion of Iraq was planned secretly in the Department of War (the Pentagon) at least a decade before it occurred. I was saddened and spiritually disturbed because this was the first time I was witnessed death and destruction on a global scale. It was around this same time that I became aware that my spirit guide was leading me in the direction of wisdom.

Michael Moore released *Fahrenheit 9/11* which convinced me even more that colonial patriarchy (or U.S. capitalism) is rationalized death. Millions of innocent lives were lost in the war, and business continued as usual. America, along with the rest of the world, has not been the same since then. The Patriot Act was signed, and the U.S. Department of Homeland Security was created. At that point, I felt the white world was at war with the black and brown world. The so-called "war on terror" was actually a war on the oppressed.

I decided to focus most of my attention on my community. I was now looking for ways to serve Little Haiti. I knew by serving the Haitian community, I would have reconnected with the people and found my way in the process. On October 29, 2002, while watching corporate news, I saw women and children jumped off a boat positioned on a 50-foot wooden freighter and rush the streets of Miami. Many of them were dressed in their Sunday's best fleeing hopelessness and poverty. The images were played over and over on the local and national news. The people were arrested and treated like criminals. The children, mostly girls, were put in a detention center. The wet foot, dry foot policy didn't apply to them because the Bush administration changed its policy on Haitian refugees to discourage a "feared mass exodus" from Haiti. I was pissed. I was determined then to speak out on the plight of the Haitian people. Jeb Bush, the governor of Florida at that time, claimed the war against terrorism was the reason they were tough on the Haitian people.

I reached out to Marleine Bastien, a fierce community leader and women's rights advocate in Little Haiti, to add my voice in the protest against this inhuman treatment of children. We went to the Haitian radio stations to ask the people to join us in protesting this cruel treatment. We organized a successful protest. Thousands of people joined us.

During the protest, I met a white man named Eric Simpson, who was very soft-spoken and seemed very tender. He had a booth where he sold books of revolutionary leaders like Malcolm X, Fidel Castro, Thomas Sankara, Nelson Mandela, etc. He told me he was a young socialist and the name of his political organization was the Socialist Workers Party. I was now 23 years old wanted to understand the invasion of Iraq, the role of the UN Peacekeepers in Haiti, and global poverty. He told me the reason why the Haitian people are not treated like the Cuban refugees is that the U.S. government is racist and capitalism like colonialism thrive on the oppression of black people. The solution was a socialist revolution. He knew about the Haitian revolution and the history of the U.S. intervention in Haiti.

This was the first time I met a white man who was not only a socialist but also very knowledgeable about world events. He gave me a book titled *Malcolm X Speaks to Young People* as a gift. After reading the book, Eric and I became friends. Malcolm X opened my eyes to racism. He made me realize the American Dream was always a nightmare to the majority of Black Americans. I read speeches and thoughts of Fidel Castro as well. I also realized Fidel Castro was not this monster the corporate media was portraying him to be. He was a revolutionary leader and a patriotic man who believed socialism is better for our planet and a more humane economic system than capitalism. One of his quotes I found to be true. He asks, "They talk about the failure of socialism, but where is the success of capitalism in Africa, Asia, and Latin America?" When I read that, I thought his point was solid. Capitalism was not working in Haiti either. Ever since then, I took Malcolm X's advice to young people. I started " listening for myself, thinking for myself, so I could come to an understanding for myself."

I was working full-time as waiter's assistant at the Delano in Miami Beach, a luxury hotel built in honor of Franklin Delano Roosevelt, the racist U.S. president who bragged about changing Haiti's constitution which had previously banned white people from owning land on the island. That hotel caters to the rich and famous. I worked there for a few months and quit. I couldn't handle the arrogance of the rich white people there and the amount of food that the hotel was wasted every day. I was thinking too much about hunger that the Haitian people were experiencing and the poverty that I saw in Overtown, a marginalized neighborhood for Black Americans.

After quitting my job at the Delano Hotel, I went on a soul-searching or ancestral reconnection mission. I knew as a boy that I was destined to serve my community and people. At the same time, I needed to find a job that would give me time and money to take care of my bills. I learned quickly that the system was designed to keep black and brown people down.

I was not interested much in mundane things. I have always felt the fire of my ancestors driving me. I knew it was only through community building and service that I would've put this fire to good use and live a fulfilled life. I wanted to become a fireman because you only work three days a week; the rest of the days you could do whatever you wanted. I spoke to a few friends who were firemen. They told me that I had to be a paramedic as well. I never liked seeing blood, so right away that career was off the list. I was not fit for this type of work.

When the Seminole Hard Rock Hotel & Casino opened on May 11, 2004, some of my friends went to work there. I came across one of them who showed me his weekly paycheck as a poker dealer for $1,700 after taxes. He told me that sometimes he made more money. He advised me to apply as a poker dealer's assistant first and work my way up as a poker dealer. I was motivated by the amount of money he made a week for simply going to school for three months. Teachers and other more important professionals didn't make that kind of money. So I thought to myself, *I need this job part-time, so I can focus my energy on my mission.* Although I wasn't clear what it was yet, I felt it in my spirit. I just trusted my gut feelings and intuition.

There was a process to become a poker dealer. First, I started as a valet runner. Then I became a brush (dealer's assistant), and finally, a poker dealer. Dealing poker put me in a different chapter in my life. I knew I could do this job part-time for a long time. I was only working four days a week and still made sixteen to seventeen hundred dollars. I fell in love with the game of poker and wanted to do it as a career while I was on my journey of discovering myself and my mission.

I met a gorgeous young woman on a site called Beautiful People. She caught my attention because she wrote under her profile picture that Dr. King was her favorite hero. I was curious because she was a young Caucasian who lived all the way in Australia, and her hero was black. The conversation started on Dr. King and then transformed into a love story. I told her about Haiti. She fell in love with me and Haiti. I visited her in Australia, and she came back with me to Miami so that we could get married. I took her to volunteer for Haitian Women of Miami (Fanm). While she was volunteering, she did her own research about the current political crisis in Haiti. She became more Haitian than I was. I was not paying much attention to Haiti because I had learned the white establishment was in control of the island.

Haiti was under a brutal military occupation. The rest of the world was more concerned with the life of the rich and the famous in Hollywood. In 2004, which marked the 200th anniversary the Haitian people asserted their human rights, the white establishment didn't want Haiti to have the bicentennial celebration. President Aristide was ousted from power once again, except this time it was by Bush Jr. They used one of his former generals named Guy Phillipe to do the dirty work. He is now incarcerated in US Federal prison for allegedly trafficking drugs. She told me everything. She thought I didn't care about the suffering of Haiti because I was not moved as much as she was by the number of people the UN peacekeepers were killing. She didn't know that my journey was different, and my concern was more about finding my voice and myself in the United States.

In my mind, the Haitian people were trapped again in the fight against global white supremacy from every angle. My mission was to find a way out. Being too concerned and stressed out by the number of Haitian people being killed by the bullets of UN peacekeepers was not going to help me get clarity. What I wanted more than anything was clarity of vision.

Moving forward to 2007 and 2008, America was now involved in two wars, which were endless, according to former President Bush. This "war on terror" seemed to be a fabricated white narrative to justify the killing and assassination of freedom fighters, journalists, and the invasion of black and brown nations. The mainstream narrative was that all Muslims are terrorists, all black men in the U.S. are thugs and criminals, and all leaders from the African continent were warlords and corrupt. Africa was impoverished because of corruption; Haiti was its extension. They all needed a white savior to give them a hand up. To paraphrase Shirley Chisholm, "Racism was so universal, so widespread, and so deep-seated, that it was invisible because it was normal." I was sickened by this simple-minded and racist narratives. The average white-skinned person could not see it for themselves.

I was reading, listening, and paying attention to everything. I was hearing the pain of my black family in the United States and in Haiti, crying for justice. It was the status quo, and the people couldn't hear them. At this point, I distrusted all politicians. I was also convinced Bill Clinton was the biggest enemy of Haiti since Leclerc.

When President Obama stepped on the national stage at the Democratic National Convention in 2004, I saw a fire in him. The same fire that I saw in Dr. King when I moved to Miami on January

15, 1996. I didn't know who Senator Obama was before, but it felt like a breath of fresh air. It was the beginning of a new day and season in U.S. politics. I was certain that I was going to hear from him again. I was mostly impressed by the fact that he was uniting the people and the first politician who was both brave and humble to bring up race in the national conversation during a presidential campaign. He uttered powerfully and beautifully, "Yet even as we speak, there are those who are preparing to divide us. The spin masters and negative ad peddlers who embrace the politics of anything goes. Well, I say to them tonight, there's not a liberal America and a conservative America-- there's the United States of America. There's not a black America and a white America; there's the United States of America. The pundits like to slice-and-dice our country into Red States and Blue States; Red States for Republicans, blue States for Democrats. But I've got news for them. We worship an awesome God in the Blue States, and we don't like federal agents poking around our libraries in the Red States. We coach Little league in the Blue States and have gay friends in the Red States. There are patriots who opposed the war in Iraq and patriots who supported it. We are one people, all of us pledging allegiance to the stars and stripes, all of us defending the United States of America." After that speech, I was now a fan of Senator Obama. He was authentic and black in the highest sense of the word. I was expecting to hear back from him.

During the war in Iraq, there was a lot of money being made in security contracts in the "green zones." in Iraq. I had a friend who had just come from Haiti. He was working as a security guard for $8.00 an hour in the U.S. He was acquainted with a beautiful Haitian woman who married a white man who was connected with Halliburton. She helped him get a security contract in Iraq, starting at $100,000. The U.S. soldiers who were dying senselessly in Iraq were making less $30,000, yet a former police officer from Haiti who didn't speak English got a contract almost three times the amount the U.S. soldiers who were in danger zones.

I started to see U.S. capitalism as soulless as the European colonizers. On the international front, U.S. taxpayers were paying for two wars. Domestically, financial institutions, such as Lehman Brothers, Fannie Mae, and monsters like Bernie Madoff were playing with the savings and lives of millions through fraudulent transactions and financial Ponzi schemes. When the colonial economy, popularly known as the market economy, collapsed down in 2008, I was on a spiritual journey. I was following and listening more to my spirit. My spirit interpreted the financial collapse as the end of a rotten system which was thriving on human suffering. Like everything in life, it has a beginning and an end.

I saw the 2008 financial collapse as a sign that U.S. capitalism needed a check-up. This economic system, which is nothing but a mutation of colonial slavery, was on its deathbed gasping for air. I was glad to see the monster dying naturally instead of our beautiful planet earth. When the economists claimed that those companies were too big to fail and they got bailed out with our tax dollars, it was around that time I was beginning to see our collective future clearer and better. I saw U.S. capitalism for what it really was -- colonial patriarchy, a grave threat to humanity and world peace. I foresaw women rising everywhere as a result of this failing system. I was preparing myself for the future.

When I heard of President Obama again, he was now a presidential candidate. Like always, his presidential announcement was not only inspiring but also historical. For it set in motion the momentum for his presidential victory in November 2008. I didn't believe he was going to win. Many black people didn't believe he was going to win either. I started believing in him after the Clintons leaked a soundbite video of a sermon his former pastor, Jeremiah Wright, delivered about the history of American slavery and racism. The corporate media ran with the story and played only the snippets of the sermon where he said, "not God bless America, God damn America." Seeing how Senator Obama defended himself and his pastor made me believe he was chosen by destiny to lead.

A picture of him dressing in a Muslim outfit was also leaked to paint him as a terrorist sympathizer. Hillary forced him to disown Louis Farrakhan, which he did, but he defended his pastor. He crafted another historic speech in the middle of the controversy titled " A More Perfect Union" to address the American people. He was now the first presidential candidate that I am aware of since Abraham Lincoln to talk about race relations in U.S. history. Prior to that, it was not the politically correct thing to do.

I watched the campaign carefully. I was eager to hear how he was going to bring the country back together while also tackling this divisive five-hundred-pound gorilla in America's closet. I was aligning myself for what I felt was my calling and destiny. I was watching the campaign carefully but from a distance. I was preparing myself and clearing my vision. My heartbeat was with the people in Haiti. I heard their voices and felt their pain. The white establishment was strangling Haiti peacefully, and the people were dying silently. Their voices were being stifled by their enemies. The only way I believed they were going to be saved was through enlightened leadership. A leader would have to emerge like in 1801 and 1804. I didn't see that leader rising from Haiti because they carried too much pain and trauma to lead them to the next glorious chapter of Haiti's history. When I looked within myself, I saw that I was the leader. I felt that my first priority to be effective and successful was to emerge in the United States by introducing myself to the American people and then going back to Haiti to share the light and healing with the people. I knew and felt in my spirit that my mission was to pick up where my ancestors left off, which is scary and monumental. That's the reason I always felt that I was raised where Jean-Jacques Dessalines fell, leaving his energy and blood a minute from the house I lived in. As Sherry Mitchell wrote in her powerful book, *The Sacred Instructions*, " A warrior is aware of their obligations toward all life, past, present, and future, and takes care to develop discipline in their walk upon the Earth. Warriors like these don't just emerge. They are carefully cultivated in fertile ground and nurtured into being." I was always aware of my obligations toward all life. I don't know why that is, but I think it's mostly because my sins were washed with the blood of Emperor Dessalines. I was in a good and fertilized ground. I was prepared and molded by our Creator before birth for this endeavor.

When Senator Obama addressed the American people on race relations, he did a wonderful job. I became very proud of him after that. I knew then he was destined to be the next president. A better speech could not have been delivered to soothe the hearts and minds of the American people at the time. The U.S. economy was falling apart. The speech was truthful, and the delivery was refreshing and beautiful worded, but the part I find to be the most powerful was when he told the American people:

"I can no more disown him (his pastor) than I can disown the black community. I can no more disown him than I can disown my white grandmother — a woman who helped raise me, a woman who sacrificed again and again for me, a woman who loves me as much as she loves anything in this world, but a woman who once confessed her fear of black men who passed her by on the street, and who on more than one occasion has uttered racial or ethnic stereotypes that made me cringe. These people are a part of me. And they are part of America, this country that I love.

"Some will see this as an attempt to justify or excuse comments that are simply inexcusable. I can assure you it is not. I suppose the politically safe thing to do would be to move on from this episode and just hope that it fades into the woodwork. We can dismiss Reverend Wright as a crank or a demagogue, just as some have dismissed Geraldine Ferraro, in the aftermath of her recent statements, as harboring some deep-seated bias. But race is an issue that I believe this nation cannot afford to ignore right now. We would be making the same mistake that Reverend Wright made in his offending sermons about America — to simplify and stereotype and amplify the negative to the point that it distorts reality.

"The fact is that the comments that have been made and the issues that have surfaced over the last few weeks reflect the complexities of race in this country that we've never really worked through — a part of our union that we have not yet made perfect. And if we walk away now, if we simply retreat into our respective corners, we will never be able to come together and solve challenges like health care or education or the need to find good jobs for every American.

Understanding this reality requires a reminder of how we arrived at this point. As William Faulkner once wrote, 'The past isn't dead and buried. In fact, it isn't even past.' We do not need to recite here the history of racial injustice in this country. But we do need to remind ourselves that so many of the disparities that exist between the African-American community and the larger American community today can be traced directly to inequalities passed on from an earlier generation that suffered under the brutal legacy of slavery and Jim Crow."

Being convinced now that Senator Obama was going to be elected, I was now getting prepared to play my part in ushering this new birth of freedom on this Earth as he said at the launching of his historic presidential campaign in Chicago in 2008. I felt destiny calling me, and I saw a future of endless possibility stretching before me. I didn't believe that the political establishment was a platform for it. There was too much toxicity and spiritual sickness in Washington. Space and the vibration were too colonized, but I still praised and respected Obama for having the courage, self-confidence, and audacity to go in that environment to change this toxic political culture. A culture that promotes enslavement and death to the majority of black and brown people. My vision was about building a grassroots movement. I trusted his intellect and vision, but I was focused on my vision.

Haitian history has taught me that America was not a post-colonial nation. The white establishment in the United States does not think and behave differently from the French colonists who were expelled from Hayti. They are as arrogant and racists as the French. From what I observed on my journey from Hayti to Miami, Euro-American leaders are a mutated version of their ancestors. They are racist colonizers. They are Europeans in spirit. They believe in upholding whiteness more than anything else. They don't believe in universal human liberty and rights.

When they utter noble words such as liberty and equality, they mean for whites only. In their hearts, they are plotting death and the enslavement of black and brown people. In order to live in harmony with these tyrants, as the Haitian heroes called them, they have to be transformed or healed from their spiritual wounds.

Whites are deeply wounded spiritually and not even aware of it. Their history and record since they landed on the shores of the Americas is the only proof we need to understand the depth of this sickness. So when former Senator Obama was elected 44th president of the United States, I was shocked and excited. I was happy to see what seemed almost impossible to become a reality. But I also knew there would be backlash after his presidency unless white people made history too.

One of my Haitian ancestors, Baron de Vastey, taught me that "whites would never abandon their desire to compete with blacks. The scale has always tipped towards their side and not the other." So aside from my personal vision of the future, which I felt was aligned with President Obama, I was also preparing for the backlash.

The sickness I observed from white America's culture was the way white women were treated. They were not honored and respected. Most of them have low self-esteem because they were taught as early as four or five years old that their physical beauty was more important than their inner beauty. The intelligent ones were not (and still aren't) promoted or edified unless they are contributing to the brutality and preserving of colonial patriarchy. The most popular ones are Ayn Rand, Margareth Thatcher, Madeleine Albright, and Hillary Clinton. Since they have closer contact with white men more than any other groups, they become a reflection of them. Everything they do is calculated and without spirit. They are the first victims and beneficiaries of patriarchy and sickness. With the exception of Mary Wollstonecraft, Hellen Keller, and Anaïs Nin, most of the outspoken or independent white women in modern history have often been a female version of their husbands, an echo of white male arrogance. On the aggregate, they are the most passionate supporters and allies of colonial patriarchy. Although the first American feminist was a black woman named Elizabeth Freeman, aka Mumbet, and the first self-made female millionaire was a black woman named Madame C.J. Walker, they took the credit as the pioneers of the women's movement in the United States. They are often as resentful and hateful as white men when black people make strides in this colonial culture. To fully understand this history, we have to go back and study the Suffrage Movement.

When black American men got the right to vote before white women, Elizabeth Cady Stanton, one of the prominent leaders of women's suffrage, was angry and resentful. She wrote in a popular abolitionist paper called the National Anti-Slavery Standard, "But now that the Negro was free, now, as the celestial gate to civil rights is slowly moving on its hinges, it becomes a serious question whether we had better stand aside and see 'Sambo' walk into the kingdom first. Who could be sure that if the Negro men secured the ballot, they might not become "an added power to hold us at bay? ...Why should the African prove more just and generous than his Saxon compeers? And what about the two million black women in the South? What would their freedom mean if they did not obtain civil rights and the right to vote? In fact, it is better to be the slave of an educated white man, than of a degraded, ignorant black one." She was blinded by arrogance and racial prejudices by colonial patriarchy. Thank God there was a Frederick Douglass.

At the American Equal Rights Association Convention held in New York City on May 12, 1869, he responded to her, " there is no name greater than that of Elizabeth Cady Stanton in the matter of women's rights and equal rights, but my sentiments are tinged a little against the revolution. There was in the address to which I allude the employment of certain names, such as " Sambo," and the gardener, and the bootblack, and the daughters of Jefferson and Washington and other daughters. I must say that I asked what difference there is between the daughters of Jefferson and Washington and other daughters. I must say that I do not see how anyone can pretend that there is the same urgency in giving the ballot to a woman as to the negro. With us, the matter is a question of life and death, at least, in fifteen States of the Union. When women, because they are women, are hunted down through the cities of New York and New Orleans; when they are dragged from their houses and hung upon lamps-posts; when their children are torn from their arms, and their brains dashed out upon the pavement; when they are objects of insults and outrage at every turn; when they are in danger of having their homes burnt down over their heads; when their children are not allowed to enter schools; then they will have an urgency to obtain the ballot equal to our own."

Someone uttered from the audience, "Is that not all true about black women?" Douglass replied, "Yes, yes, yes; it is true of the black woman, but not because she is a woman, but because she is black." Knowing about this racial tension in the suffrage movement and in almost every social movement throughout U.S. history, I was now preparing myself for the future.

After Obama's victory, I became very attentive to him. I saw him as a man fit for this time and century. When he said in his 2009 inauguration address, "The time has come to set aside childish things. The time has come to reaffirm our enduring spirit; to choose our better history; to carry forward that precious gift, that noble idea passed on from generation to generation: the God-given promise that all are equal, all are free, and all deserve a chance to pursue their full measure of happiness." I interpreted it as a direct message to get to work. I knew there was a generation of powerful white men who weren't going to put aside childish things.

Days after Obama was elected President, the corporate media gave reality TV star Donald Trump, a microphone to express his venoms and bigotry. To them, Donald Trump was a joke. He claimed President Obama was born in Kenya and that his presidency was illegitimate. Thus, the birther movement was born. Personally, I was only interested in the glorious future that a new generation of American was about to invent. I trusted President Obama's vision and judgment fully on January 29, 2009, when I saw he signed into law the equal pay for equal work bill popularly known as the Lilly Ledbetter Fair Pay Act less than two weeks after he took the oath of the office. He also established a White House Council on Women and Girls on March 11, 2009. I knew then that President Obama was about to bust the white bubble and piss a lot of white people off. I sensed he was going to shift the culture and upgrade U.S. democracy, which, prior to his presidency, was only a colonial democracy.

I noticed that the majority of people who voted for President Obama were millennials. So, on November 25, 2009, I established the Millennials Project to build a grassroots movement to end the culture of violence against women and advocate for gender equality. I picked November 25 because it was designated by the UN in 1999 as the International Day for the Elimination of Violence Against Women. Historically, the date is based on the date three women, and political activists, better known as the Mirabal sisters, were raped and murdered in the Dominican Republic by dictator Rafael Trujillo. He is the same man who slaughtered more than ten thousand Haitian men, women, and children in the Dominican Republic in the spring of 1938. His plan was to whiten the country. With President Obama being bold and ready to help shift this global culture and raise awareness on women's issues, I felt the date was perfect to start this initiative as a son of Haiti.

A few weeks before establishing the Millennials Project on November 25, 2009, I attended a community gathering to celebrate Abraham Lincoln's 200th birthday. I did so to connect with community leaders and introduce myself as an emerging leader. From the start, I wanted to become a leader in Miami using only my ancestral fire. All the important community leaders were there, from political to non-profit. The theme was "Lincoln, Miami and the American Dream." The event was sponsored by two prestigious white institutions in Miami, the Knight Foundation and the Miami Foundation. Those two foundations as I came to find out on my journey later are like the Republican and Democratic Parties of goodwill. They are two wings of the same bird. They give "grants" to all the initiatives in the city. Professor Henry Louis Gates was the keynote speaker, and Mayor Carlos Alvarez and Alonzo Mourning were among some of the panelists.

From the beginning of the event, I was insulted. A white woman by the name of Eileen Mackevich began the event with this opening statement," We are delighted to bring the celebration of Abraham Lincoln's life and legacy to Miami, a city that embraces and celebrates its cultural and ethnic diversity perhaps more than any other American city. It's fitting that we gather in Miami to talk about his life and about the American Dream. In so many ways, Abraham Lincoln exemplified that dream, and during his life worked tirelessly to make the American Dream a worthy and attainable pursuit for generations to come." And then, Mayor Carlos Alvarez added, "If Abraham Lincoln visited Miami-Dade County today, I think he would be very proud to see that his legacy of equality among people is alive and well."

I was boiling inside. I couldn't believe what I had just heard. Abraham Lincoln, a racist white man who didn't believe in social and political equality between black and white people, was being praised and painted as a universal human rights champion. I was like, what an insult to the intelligence of black people? I felt a little better when Professor Henry Louis Gates spoke. He said, in the most diplomatic manner, what I was feeling inside. He called Abraham Lincoln for what he was, a good white man for his time but a racist like all the other U.S. presidents., in my opinion.

After the event was over, I made it my mission to meet all the influential leaders starting with the president of the Knight Foundation, Alberto Ibargüen, the white man who seemed to be the godfather of Miami. As he was walking to his car with his partner, I walked up to him and whispered that I have a great idea about improving American democracy that I would like to share with him. He stopped and gave me his secretary's email to contact her for an appointment. At that time, I had a foggy vision of my mission, and the organization was not incorporated yet. I met him on November 1, 2009 and established the Millennials Project on November 25, 2009.

I spoke to my mother, who was in Haiti, right after the organization was established and told her I had found my mission and planned on spending the rest of my life advocating for the justice of women. I spoke to my father and everyone else who was important in my life a week after. Almost all of them didn't take me seriously with the exception of my mother and my little brother. I told all the women leaders in Miami, including Marleine Bastien, that I was embarking on this endeavor. She thought it was a good initiative because there wasn't any organization in Miami initiated by a man to support the women's movement.

By December 2009, everyone in my circle knew about this new initiative that I had started. I felt destiny calling and saw, as President Obama said, "a future of endless possibility stretching before me." I understood exactly what he meant when he said, "If you sense, as I sense, that the time is now to shake off our slumber, and slough off our fear, and make good on the debt we owe past and future generations, then I am ready to take up the cause and march with you and work with you. Together, starting today, let us finish the work that needs to be done, and usher in a new birth of freedom on this Earth." I was ready to help usher this new birth of freedom. Too many of my brothers and sisters were suffering back in my native land in Hayti, Miami, and around the world.

On January 11, 2010, I emailed Alberto Ibargüen's secretary to share the idea of improving American democracy with him. She responded right away and asked me to call the office. I called her, and she scheduled an appointment for February 1, 2010 to meet with Mr. Alberto. The next day, January 12, 2010, my beloved homeland of Haiti was struck by a devastating 7.0 earthquake, killing more than a quarter of a million people. I was in the breakroom at my job at the Seminole Hard Rock Hotel & Casino watching CNN when Wolf Blitzer broke the story. That same night, Anderson Cooper flew to Port-au-Prince with Wyclef Jean to capitalize on the story. The next day, white journalists and media outlets were all over Haiti whitesplaining the tragedy. Not one journalist explained in context why Haiti was so impoverished or gave their audience the chronological order of how Haiti was isolated, and her economy was strangled. I believe Anderson Cooper spoke briefly about the role of the U.S. government in supporting the thirty-year rule of the Duvaliers, but he didn't speak of the price of independence the Haitian people were forced to pay nor the brutal U.S. occupation of Haiti that started in 1915.

Black bodies were everywhere. The media wasn't educating the public on what was going on. The only person who was more honest about the situation was Dr. Sanjay Gupta. He reported the story from the perspective of a doctor. He was speaking to Oprah when I heard him say to the American people, "The U.S. Army was in charge of Toussaint L'Ouverture Airport, and they didn't allow medicine such as anesthesia to amputate the Haitian people whose arms and legs were broken from the tragedy. They were amputated without anesthesia."

I was moved and emotionally disturbed by the images I saw on those networks. First responders went to help look for victims with the relief efforts. In Miami, white saviors were all over the city. There was a fundraiser organized by a white person for Haiti in every corner of Miami. Hillary Clinton, who was then secretary of state, was more concerned about the gold rush than anything else. Bill Clinton, who was then appointed as the "special envoy" to Haiti by the UN the same year Obama was sworn in as the president of the United States, was silent. He didn't say a word when the earthquake struck the island, killing all people. He waited until April 1, 2010 to give a calculated and half-hearted apology to Congress about his role in starving the Haitian people. His apology was an insult to injury. He said, "Since 1981, the United States has followed a policy, until the last year or so when we started rethinking it, that we rich countries that produce a lot of food should sell it to poor countries and relieve them of the burden of producing their own food. So, thank goodness, they can leap directly into the industrial era. It has not worked. It may have been good for some of my farmers in Arkansas, but it has not worked. It was a mistake. It was a mistake that I was a part of. I am not pointing the finger at anybody. I did that. I have to live every day with the consequences of the lost capacity to produce a rice crop in Haiti to feed those people because of what I did. Nobody else."

At the time, I was praying and felt in my heart that my mother survived this deadly earthquake. In my heart, it felt like she survived, but my mind was in doubt. The last time I spoke to her was after I initiated the Millennials Project. I heard from my brother almost two weeks after the earthquake. He told me everyone was okay. My mother was outside the house and survived. The moment she felt the earth shaking, she laid on her stomach on the ground. I felt relief and decided to go to Haiti to start building the movement.

There was no commercial flight from Miami to Haiti, so I booked one from Miami to the Dominican Republic the day after my meeting with Mr. Alberto Ibargüen, the president of the Knight Foundation. Then I crossed over by bus to Haiti. I interpreted the earthquake as a natural revolution. Haiti was being strangled and suffocated by the white world, so the earthquake was a natural explosion to birth a new beginning, a new day. There was too much pain and suffering on the island; the earth had to scream.

I purposefully went to my meeting with Mr. Alberto to the meeting with a young white man from Chicago named Brian Jackson. How we connected is another interesting story of its own. He was volunteering for Planting Peace, an organization founded by Aaron Jackson to deworm children in Haiti. He was named a CNN Hero in 2007 for his work in Haiti.

After his interview with CNN, he was contacted by an executive from Goldman Sachs who asked him for his 501c3 status. He was excited and thought that he was going to get a big check from that racist bank. He received a check for $100.00 dollars. He was disappointed that a bank like Goldman Sachs, which was bailed out with billions of our tax dollars, asked for his tax-exempt status before giving him one hundred dollars.

While I was calling his office to tell him not to cash the check, I couldn't find him. Brian kept answering his office phone. This is how Brian and I became connected. We spoke over the phone a few times. I told him that I am an advocate for gender equality and that I believe our generation should stand with women in this struggle for justice. He agreed, and we were acquainted and became friends. He moved from Chicago to South Florida at the beginning of 2010, and that's how I ended up taking him to the meeting with Alberto.

When I walked in Mr. Alberto's fancy office on the top floor of one of the tallest buildings in Downtown Miami, the first thing he noticed was Brian Jackson. Miami is very segregated. Black-skinned people and white-skinned people live in their own "district," as it is called now. They don't mingle with each other as much. So he was surprised to see Brian, who was a white male with me at the meeting. He asked, "How do you guys know each other?" Brian answered him because I knew the reason why he asked, and I was going to tell him how. I was wearing a Ralph Lauren Polo with the Haitian flag on it to raise funds for relief efforts. He brought up Hillary's name for no reason, telling me of the work she was doing in the inner city.

While he was taking me on tour around his office, I told him my idea of improving American democracy. I told him that I believed women are finer and morally superior to men and that if he invests in them, everyone will be better off. I told him that because I felt guided by the spirit of the ancestors, and they wanted me to tell him that. He paused for a few seconds and replied, " I don't believe in that. Do you mean Hillary?" At that point, I felt like he gave me inside information. He told me who the white establishment was going to select after President Obama's presidency. I didn't tell who I meant because I wasn't referring to a particular woman. I had a vision of women rising and knew President Obama and First Lady Michelle were going to shift the culture in that sense.

I gave him a look which expressed my sentiments when he brought up Hillary's name. He quickly realized the meeting was not about what he thought. The Knight Foundation is a private foundation with 2.6 billion dollars. Most people who get the opportunity to meet him, I assume to tell him things he wants to hear. As I came to find out in my journey later, the mission of the Knight Foundation and all the established institutions are to keep and protect the status quo. In Miami, the members of the status quo are Jewish and Cuban. Blacks and other ethnic groups are marginalized and impoverished.

When I told him I was flying to Haiti the next day, he asked, "What are you going to do there?" I answered softly, "Help with relief efforts." He gave me his cell number to contact him when I get back. When I did get back from Haiti, he was nowhere to be found.

I arrived in Haiti on February 2, 2010, heart-wrenched by the sheer poverty and misery I saw in Pont-Rouge, the community I left as a boy. More than twenty thousand people were jammed up in what was once a military aviation in front of Emperor Dessalines' monument, looking like slaves.

I slept in a makeshift tent for two days to connect with the people and see what was happening for myself. I was inspired by their Indigenous spirit of resilience; they were ready to move on with their lives in spite of the traumas and the hardships they were facing. They complained about the absence of government officials and the NGO, which hadn't visit them since January 12. They slept in tents with babies as old as four months. It was really painful to see. The conditions were beyond slavish and miserable. Mothers and fathers were begging for help, and children were crying for food, water, and safety. Chelsea Clinton's description was accurate in the heartfelt memo she wrote to "Mom and Dad," which was leaked by WikiLeaks in 2016. "Haitians want to help themselves and want the international community to help them help themselves. This sounds obvious but wasn't to some of the UN and the international NGO (INGO) folks I ran across. The UN people I encountered were frequently out of touch, anachronistic at best, and arrogant and incompetent at worst. If we do not quickly change the organization management, accountability and delivery on the ground, we could quite conceivably confront tens of thousands of children's deaths by diarrhea, dysentery, typhoid and other water-related diseases in the near future."

Chelsea was referring to the camp in Pont-Rouge by the Emperor Dessalines' monument. The camp was an aviation turned into a park after Bill Clinton invaded the island in 1994, which is now named after Father Jean-Marie Vincent, a pro-democracy priest who was assassinated after President Aristide was violently overthrown in the '90s. I am not sure how long after I left she went to the camp, but whoever brought her there didn't explain to her that she was walking on sacred ground or that Pont Rouge was the area where the greatest black warrior who ever lived was assassinated.

The people were traumatized by the death of their loved ones and hardened by the brutal poverty and the oppression of the United Nations. The tents they were sleeping in were made with bedsheets. If it rained, they were in serious trouble. I was pissed at the NGO and the Haitian leaders. It was at that moment I realized Haiti was under the complete control of the Clintons and the United Nations. The UN peacekeepers were patrolling the island with the same weapons U.S. soldiers in Iraq were using after Saddam Hussein was overthrown.

I felt a sense of terror and fearlessness watching foreign soldiers with this deadly armament driving around Dessalines' monument in Pont-Rouge. Dessalines' secretary told us in 1804 that if we ever see one white man with a gun on Haytian soil, the whole country needs to unite and get ready for war. Now there were thousands of white men in Haiti with heavy armament.

When I left Haiti at the dawn of 1996, I did feel that energy of terror, but it was not very intense. I was not intimidated by their presence. Instead, my conviction was strengthened. I decided to knock on the doors of all the NGOs in Haiti at that time. They were all stationed at the MINUSTAH Logistics Base near the airport. MINUSTAH is a French acronym for "United Nations Peacekeeping Mission in Haiti" and was formally established in Haiti on June 1, 2004, right after President Aristide was ousted again for asking France to pay $21 billion in restitution to Haiti for the 90 million gold francs the Haitian people were forced to pay for their independence on 1825. I was allowed on the base only because I had a U.S. passport and was accompanied by Brian Jackson.

I spoke to representatives from organizations, such as the UN Children's Fund (UNICEF), UN Refugee Agency (UNHRC), International Organization for Migration (IOM), Red Cross, World Health Organization and World Food Program about the conditions of women and children in the camp in Pont-Rouge. None of them knew what was going on or were sympathetic to the Haitian people. They were caught up in the funds being raised. All the big organizations were competing against each other and handling the crisis in the WHITEST way possible. With the spirit of whiteness being exposed and seeing the suffering of the Haitian people, Brian Jackson said silently to himself, "I am ashamed of being white," as we were walking out of MINUSTAH Logistics Base.

The next day I brought a group of women leaders with me to the meeting at the MINUSTAH Logistics Base. We were told to attend a French meeting. A white guy named Louis, who I assumed was French American, told me "the organization's resources dried up. There was no cache of tents waiting for distribution. Unless the American people decide to turn the tap back on, there is nothing we can do." At that point, I realized we were being played.

The following day, I organized a march of more than a thousand women to scream for justice in front of the MINUSTAH base. The next day they went to Pont-Rouge to drop some tents and brought some water for the people. After that victory, I told the women that we are in a big and long fight. "Today, we march for tents and clean water, tomorrow we will march for girls' education and women's rights to life and happiness."

There was no commercial flight from Haiti to the United States. I flew out of Haiti on February 9, 2010 in a U.S. military plane. After landing in Miami, I was determined more than ever to change the miserable condition of my brothers and sisters in Haiti. I was angry with white people. I pitied them. Their level of spiritual poverty was beyond my rationalization. I couldn't understand how white-skinned people could be so small-minded and blinded by greed and racial prejudices. I was baffled by this smallness of spirit.

The ones representing the NGOs in Haiti and the ones who were trying to make some quick money for themselves in Miami exerted the same spirit of arrogance. I didn't want to believe that what my Haytian ancestors said about the French was still relevant and applicable in 2010. My ancestral fire was LIT. This fire was felt by everyone who came in contact with me.

A year after the earthquake, the corporate media refocused its energy on other racially-motivated and sensationalized news in the U.S. Bill Clinton, Sean Penn, Donna Karen, and white saviors from almost every former colonial powers were now in the spotlight, capitalizing on the pain and suffering of the people in the name of humanitarian aid. It was like watching my mother being beaten and abused again. The only thing I could do was watching white people rationalizing it on CNN. Haiti was like a second home for Bill Clinton, a covert racist white man who appears to be decent but carries darkness in his soul that only God and probably his wife know.

I took four trips to Haiti after the earthquake. Every time I was on my way out of Haiti, the plane was always full of white people. So, to keep cool and calm, I refocused my energy on the movement in the United States. Originally, when I established the organization on November 25, 2009, my intention was to build the movement within the borders of the United States and then export it to Haiti. My thought process was if white people wanted to save Haiti, I would let them do it since they have a monopoly of intelligence and geniuses. They understand Haiti's challenges better than everyone else. My priority now was finding good and solid men to build the movement in the U.S. I didn't know how I was going to convince men like myself who have sinned against women that women's issues should be their concern. But I knew if I started by example, I would be able to engage and recruit other men.

I have always felt that the safety of women is our collective responsibility. I took one step at a time, trusting the ancestors would give me the language and empower me along the way. What I noticed was that every time I shared the vision of supporting women with a male member of the human family, he always referred me to a woman leader or organization. The majority of white men and some black men didn't understand the simple truth that women's rights are also human rights. Only the Indigenous American brother named Wayne William Snellgrove, who was kidnapped by Christian missionaries in a hospital from Canada, understood the simple and sacred responsibility.

I came across him at one of his ancestral ceremonies he facilitates to heal relations between races. He instantly understood what the movement was about. He didn't hesitate to join me when I told him that I was building a movement of men to make the community safer and better for women. Most men I came across couldn't see themselves as allies in the women's movement. Those who did support me were supporting me (not the cause) because they have a daughter. The rest didn't have a voice or seem to understand the true spirit of masculinity.

I understood the challenge was cultural right away. Being raised in a culture where women are being hyper-sexualized and rarely honored, it's easy for young men to get lost and be out of balance. As Sherry Mitchell noted in her book, *The Sacred Instructions*, "Patriarchy shifted men from their role of protecting life and turned them toward the protection of material items. They taught them to value material items more than they valued life." I am not sure when this shift happened in human history, but I have many reasons to believe it happened first on the European continent and exported throughout the rest of the world. I believe the shift took place after the first European man was kidnapped and sold into slavery, and the first European woman was burned at the stake for being witch or a healer.

Throughout European civilizations and history, I learned manhood seemed to have been measured by two things: the conquest of land and the ownership of slaves. William O Blake, the author of *The History of Slavery and The Slave Trade*, explains it pretty well. He said that "in Ancient Greece and Rome, it was considered a reproach to a man not to keep a considerable number of slaves. The first question asked respecting a person's fortune was an inquiry as to the number of his slaves." When you study European history, some of the most upright thinkers were either slaves or former slaves. Diogenes, the influential Greek philosopher who was later sold into slavery, became known for walking through the streets of Athens in the daytime with a lantern. When asked what he was looking for, he answered, "I am seeking a man. Men, I have found nowhere in Lace-daemon."

The history of masculinity or manhood in the European sense was always distorted, dark, and cruel. The white men of today, especially those born before the Black American freedom struggle in the 60s, do not think much differently from the Europeans of ancient Rome and Greece. They are, in fact, their ancestors' wildest dream. The beauty of the time we live in is we are at a crossroad right now. We have an opportunity to set afoot a new type of man, as Martin Luther King noted in his book.

The white men who I see running America's institutions right now are more European than Americans. Their closest allies are European countries and leaders. Former slave and American hero, Frederick Douglass also saw how colonial patriarchy and slavery has deeply injured men emotionally and spiritually. He wrote in his autobiography, "It is easier to raise strong children than to repair broken men." Colonial patriarchy, which is another name for slavery and death, has broken too many men in his time. It's mind-boggling to see how it evolved in the 21st century.

After the institution of slavery was disrupted by machinery and the forces of industrialization, the snake shed new skin, and anti-black racism was legalized, and the lynching of black men and the raping of black women became a political strategy. This sickness of spirit started in 1865 and continues to this day. The last three Senators who attempted to make lynching a federal hate crime in the United States were Kamila Harris, Cory Booker, and Tim Scott on June 30, 2018.

Now brothers and sisters, think how deeply wounded and sick we are as people in America. When President Obama was elected in 2009, the white press said that America was post-racial, but in reality, America was not even post-colonial. Slavery is legal in United States prisons. They wanted us to believe Obama's victory was proof that race-based oppression was finally over two hundred and thirty-three years after the enlightened Thomas Jefferson discovered the self-evident truth that "ALL MEN are created equal." As a son of Hayti, I didn't buy it. This is why I took off my bedroom slippers and hit the road. I was preparing myself for this dark moment which is a pure reflection of the white colonizers in America.

Too many ancestors told me about the spirit of the Europeans. My Haitian ancestors were the only ones to avenge the crimes and bestiality they committed on this continent upon their arrival. I don't want to outline them in this book. To understand this history, you have to read anything written by or about the pioneer anti-colonial thinker, Baron De Vastey. He published *Le Système colonial dévoilé* in 1814 to educate white people about Hayti and the barbarity they were dealing with before the French colonists whom he described as odious tyrants. This book was hidden by the white establishment for two centuries. It was recently translated in English by a white historian as "the colonial system unveiled." I highly recommend this classic work.

As I was building this movement at the grassroots level one man at a time, the political establishment began to pay attention to me. I was fueled by ancestral fire and my anger for how white people exploited my brothers and sisters in Haiti after the earthquake was turned into fuel to keep me going against all odds. I was unstoppable. I was one man determined to transform Miami. With the re-election of President Obama in 2012, I was certain the white establishment was going to shove Hillary down our throats.

President Obama said in his second inauguration address, "My fellow Americans, we are made for this moment, and we will seize it together--so long as we seize it together. We are true to our creed when a little girl born into the bleakest poverty knows that she has the same chance to succeed as anybody else because she is an American; she is free, and she is equal, not just in the eyes of God but also in our own." It was clear to me that I was on the same page as President Obama. We were destined to meet for the sake of history. I kept introducing myself to community leaders, but no one seemed to fully understand the gravity of the work that I was doing. I got disappointed a few times by black women who were, unfortunately, unable to see my true intention because of the traumas and pain they accumulated in their own journey into womanhood. That didn't stop and alter my vision. Instead, I opened my first office at a building in little Haiti called Jean-Jacques Dessalines' Building before it was gentrified to use the language of a white establishment.

The country seemed like it was getting ready to shift culturally. The Women's Funds of Miami was hosting a monthly meeting with community leaders to discuss ideas on how to reduce and prevent violence against women in the city. I was always the only man in the meeting. I didn't care because I was on a mission and I felt it was important for me to be there. I told the women in the meeting that I was building a movement to help end this culture of violence against women and to refer any good men they knew to help me raise awareness of the cause. The attendees were mostly white and Spanish women. Some of the older white women seemed to have been bothered at one point by my presence, because of the images and stereotypes they had of black men were being shattered. They weren't used to seeing a black man like President Obama sitting in the highest office of the land and seeing Haytian man who is at the bottom of social hierarchy in Miami standing fully upright. Everyone attended the meeting had their own agendas.

At this point, I was being watched by the establishment in Miami. The private foundations were giving "grants" to the community. They sent their agents to watch and connect with leaders throughout Miami. There was a meeting hosted by the Knight Foundation every month for community leaders. I attended those meetings as well to share my vision and the movement I was building in the city.

The Community director of the Knight Foundation didn't know then that I had met his boss. He invited me to a meeting with the hope of giving me a "grant." When he found out the movement I was building was for all women, not just black women, he politely kicked me out of his office.

The Women's Fund announced a grant to help organizations end the culture of violence against women. I applied for the grants. Three women came to my office at the Jean-Jacques Dessalines building for an interview before the grant. One black woman, a white woman, and a Hispanic woman. From the start of the interview, I knew the black and Hispanic women were just pawns. They didn't have any saying in deciding whether I was going to get the grant or not. The old white woman's behavior was so abhorrent, I regretted not showing a picture of Emperor Jean-Jacques Dessalines at the end of the interview. During the interview, she said that she has been doing this type of work for twenty-five years and had never met a man who was doing what I was doing as if my motivation was to get the ten thousand dollars grant. She walked out of the building like she was too good to be in Little Haiti.

The next day I got an email from the Women's Fund requesting me to send them a copy of my letter from the Florida Division of Consumer Services for soliciting donations. I didn't have it on time to fax it to them, and they didn't give me the grant. I was forced to use my savings to continue building the movement until there was nothing left. Almost as soon as I had begun to drain the savings account, it was completely empty. I couldn't pay the monthly office rent for the office or the organization's phone line. My board members couldn't see the reason why I continued to invest time and energy in the cause. I wasn't getting financial support from the community.

Although I wasn't getting support from the Women's Fund. I decided to go to another community meeting on domestic violence prevention. This time, the special guest was a Cuban American woman named Yvon Mesa, the executive director of Miami-Dade County Community Action and Human Services Department. After introducing myself to the people who were at the meeting, she told me that she heard about my work in the community and was trying to contact me. We spoke briefly after the meeting was over about forming a partnership with Miami-Dade County to lead the conversation on domestic violence. We scheduled to meet a month later at her office in Coral Gables.

At first, I hesitated about forming the partnership with a government entity because I didn't want the movement to be tainted, knowing Miami politics was too corrupt. I agreed to form the partnership after I realized I didn't have anything to lose since I was having difficulties paying for my own office, but I made a sacred agreement to remain true to the cause and myself. She took me around the building to pick an office and promised that we were going to apply for a federal grant program which specifically addressed "children and youth experiencing domestic violence and sexual assault and engaging men and boys as allies." On September 25, 2014, I signed a Memorandum of Understanding with Miami-Dade County, Community Action and Human Services Department, a political subdivision of the State of Florida. While I was signing the Memorandum, she told me the only reason I was signing this partnership was that she couldn't find a Cuban man who was doing this type of work. I told her that the main reason I am doing this work is to change the way men who look like me are portrayed in the mainstream culture.

From the beginning of the partnership, I didn't trust Cuban politicians. I had a feeling that I was going to be used. They saw that I felt very strongly about the safety and well-being of women. Since they were working in a corrupt system, their plan was to make me do the work for free. At this point in my journey, I didn't care either because the mission was bigger than me and Miami-Dade County. Coincidently, a week after I signed the partnership with Miami-Dade County; I received a grant in the amount of $5,000.00 from the Knight Foundation through Miami Foundation. The grant was for programming that promotes healthy manhood to help prevent domestic violence, sexual assault, bullying, and homophobia.

I signed the partnership with the County in September 2014. I moved in the government building the first week of February 2015. My office was next to the late Johnnie Cochran's office from what I was told. The prominent Black American lawyer who represented O.J. Simpson during his trial. The building is located in the heart of Coral Gables, an area where they are literally no black residents. I went to the office on Monday thru Thursday from 10:00 a.m. to 5:00 p.m. using my own funds for transportation, food, and even flyers. I had to use my own money to print them.

One of the responsibilities of the Millennials Project was to facilitate a monthly meeting for men on domestic violence prevention, sexual assault, and human trafficking, and a quarterly workshop for youth (boys and girls). The U.S. Department of Justice (Office on Violence Against Women) released the federal grant on February 6, 2015 for a total of $750,000 with $350,000 being reserved for engaging men projects. Applicants were encouraged to submit a letter of registration to the Department of Justice by February 26, 2015. All applications were due by 11:59 p.m. Eastern Standard Time (EST) on March 19th, 2015. The grant award period would last for 36 months.

The executive directors asked one question for the grant proposal: Why is it important for men to stand as allies against domestic violence?

My answer was the Millennials Project was founded with the belief that men should only use their weight to lift women up, not to abuse them. I don't think that's the answer they were waiting for. However, that's the answer I felt compelled to give to those two Cuban women. They asked me to elaborate. I didn't. Exactly before the deadline, they submitted the grant, which, according to them, was almost guaranteed.

While I was in the building making new connections and meeting new members, I felt like an outsider who had just invaded a Cuban platform. There was no harmony and synchronicity. The women in charge were always either on vacation or applying for grants. Money seemed to have been the biggest issue. There was not enough money to do anything. With the $ 5000.00 grant I received from the white Foundation, I used it to keep the organization moving until I got the federal grant for $350,000 on October 1.

I attended every event and gathering to connect with men in the community. I met almost every leader in Miami. The ones I didn't meet either weren't involved in a significant way or failed to impact the community in a positive away. I was preaching the gospel of safety for women to all men in the community.

As I engaged men in this conversation, I learned a lot from everyone. I learned a lot from white people, specifically from white males. I learned that nine out of ten white people who live in Miami either are prejudiced, racist, or tribalist. They all have a racist uncle, grandfather, or grandmother. This is what I found out when I started talking about the work that I did in the community. They were shocked or surprised to see a man of black skin doing this type of work.

The wisdom and insights that I gained from this journey are priceless. I met men from all four corners of the city. I was fired up and ready to lead this historic movement. President Obama, at the highest level, was raising the bar on masculinity. At the grassroots level, I was building the foundational structure for the movement. I was exerting all my energy on building the movement.

The monthly meeting I was facilitating every month wasn't attracting many men. First, it was located in my office; second, the topic was boring; third, prominent men like Warren Buffet, Richard Branson, Jimmy Carter weren't speaking out yet for women's rights or leaning in as Sherryl Sandberg described her campaign to engage men. A vast majority of men, for the most part, were not yet interested in having a conversation on women's rights and safety. So, I had to invent a way to be creative in my approach.

Knowing the white establishment was going to be behind Hillary, I had no choice but to make the movement a success. I didn't trust the Cuban politicians. I wasn't feeling good about the partnership with Miami-Dade County. Somehow, I felt they were going to betray me and the cause.

As I was meditating on my next move, a voice whispered in my ear, "Remember why you started this project. Do not trust anyone. The ancestors are with you but count only on yourself." After hearing that and the feeling I was experiencing, I decided to launch DADE MEN, a photo exhibit to make my mark in Miami. I was certain by then that the people in Miami's government were using me, so I took a page out of Toussaint L'ouverture' s playbook to outplay the Cuban politicians in Miami, who I assumed didn't know anything about the Haitian people.

The idea of DADE MEN was to introduce myself to the community and the men I was recruiting in the movement to end the culture of violence against women. I wanted the community to know who I was and what I was doing. Miami was the least safe city for women, according to the Miami Herald. I wanted the community to know that I was going to make the city the safest in the country if I had their support.

The monthly meeting I was facilitating wasn't successful enough, in my opinion. It was held in a government building, and you already know that nothing fun happens in government spaces. To prepare for October, which is Domestic Violence Awareness Month, I recruited twelve men from the four directions -- the black, white, yellow, and red road. I wasn't fully conscious of the reason I recruited the men from the four directions. One thing I had in mind was building a coalition of men from all socioeconomic statuses, ethnic backgrounds, and creeds.

Miami is a global city that is young and thriving. She is already known as the capital of South America. There are people coming from all the four corners of the world who live in Miami. Any impact I made in Miami would have a far-reaching effect. That was my attitude. I personally wanted to make Miami a model city in the United States, a social leader for change. I had the fire, spirit, and will to do it.

As time was approaching to hear from the government officials whether we were awarded the federal grant or not, my gut feeling told me it wasn't going to happen. The non-verbal messages I received from the staff in the building made me feel suspicious about this grant. The spirit doesn't lie. Energy doesn't deceive. Their energy and spirit told me everything before they called me in a meeting to make the announcement.

A few weeks before October 1, I was called by the director of the government agency in the conference room to inform me that we didn't get the federal grant. Although I had a feeling this was going to happen, I was devastated. I felt betrayed. I was emotionally weak. I didn't know how to express the emotional pain I was feeling. I went home and laid on the ground to get closer to Mother Earth for energy.

After laying down for thirty minutes, I started feeling a little better. I contacted my Board of Directors to inform them as well. I had no financial support or hope to keep the organization working and to sustain the movement. All I could do was follow my spirit and the spirits of my ancestors. I was raised to believe in the wisdom of our Creator when powerlessness overtakes me. When life seems a little too dark, I trust the Alpha and Omega of the Universe.

I grew up in Hayti with my mother, who believes in the African spiritual tradition, but my father follows the Western doctrine of Christianity. So I had a balance of worlds. After being consumed by powerlessness and being betrayed by the County government, I drew inspiration from the story of Job. Scriptures say, when Job was losing faith in God because he had lost his wealth, family, friends, and health, the Lord spoke out to him out of the storm: " Brace yourself like a man; I will question you, and you should answer. Would you discredit my justice? Would you condemn me to justify yourself? Do you have an arm like God's, and can your voice thunder like his? Then adorn yourself with glory and splendor and clothe yourself with honor and majesty." Those words were comforting to me. I did tremble a little for the future of the United States like Thomas Jefferson did when he realized that "God is just; and that his justice cannot sleep forever." I knew what had happened to me was unjust and what I was doing in the community was the work of God and the future.

I stood up and decided to move forward with the photography exhibit that I called DADE MEN. I carefully selected twelve men who made a positive contribution to business, arts, politics, religion or spirituality, and sports. I photographed them in different areas in Miami in black and white. After the photograph, I asked them to write a message or sacred oath on committing to use their voices or platforms to speak out for women and stand with them against all forms of violence. I used the photographs and the written messages for the exhibition. I framed them beautifully and invited the community to meet these men.

The launching of DADE MEN on October 1, 2015 was a major success. For the first time in Miami's history, a black man brought people of all colors to an event to raise awareness about domestic violence and celebrate men who are stepping up to support women. The next day, I got messages from women thanking me for the beautiful and empowering event. The status quo sent their agents in the event to investigate. I saw representatives of the government with their badges and from the two powerful white foundations. The event was the most talked about event in Miami for a few days. The media didn't highlight it. It was just spread by word of mouth.

A Cuban woman whose husband was the Miami director of the Knight Foundation emailed me and copied her husband to congratulate me. She wrote, "EVERYONE in Miami should see this photography exhibition." I followed up with her husband, but the Knight Foundation was not interested in supporting my cause.

A couple of weeks after DADE MEN, millions of dollars were dispersed to start an initiative called BME in Miami. BME stands for Black Men Engagement. I later found out the Knight Foundation gave them the grant. It was for more than six million dollars to be awarded to black male leaders in Miami and across the country to build prosperity. The next thing I know, black men were being honored and given ten thousand dollars for any project.

I was now leading the monthly men's meeting on domestic violence prevention, and DADE MEN was a success. My idea for the DADE MEN photography exhibition was to not only highlight good men and initiate the conversation among all men in the community about the roles they needed to play in improving women's lives, but to also honor one man whose words and photography impacted or inspired more people on the eve of International Women's Day for the elimination of violence against women.

November 25, almost two months after DADE MEN was launched, I received a call from a beautiful Jamaican woman whom I had met a few weeks prior who was married to a successful French man in Miami. She told me she nominated me for the $10,000 BME grant and advised me to apply. I was a little insulted at first because the grant was for a "black leader to build a prosperous community." I didn't see myself as a black leader, and the movement I was building was to build a safer community and city. I knew it was the Miami status quo using other black men to distract and divide the movement I was building. I meditated and prayed on it; then I decided to apply for the grant. I said to myself, "The movement is not about me, so any amount of money I receive will help the cause. Let me not let my ego get in the way of the success of this movement. This is bigger than me." And that's exactly what I did. I listened to my better angels and applied for the grant for the DADE MEN photography exhibition, a movement of men of all colors. Less than a few days later, I got a response stating, BME LETTER: GRANT DECLINED.

I was disappointed, but I somewhat expected the response from the BME community. I knew a white hand was pulling the string. I had also learned from history, personal observation, and experiences how white societies have divided and colonized black and brown people with the dollar bill. Malcolm X called it *dollarism*. Dr. King taught me to see black collaborators of white supremacy in a healthy way, so I was not angry with them. He wrote in his book, *Why We Can't Wait*; "Negroes are human, not superhuman. Like all people, they have differing personalities, diverse monetary interests, and varied aspirations. There are Negroes who will never fight for freedom. There are Negroes who will seek profit for themselves alone from the struggle. These facts should distress no-one. Every minority and every people has its share of opportunists, profiteers, freeloaders and escapists."

Dr. King's words helped me on my journey of discovery and healing. I learned every time I judge someone else, however misguided he or she might be, I reveal an unhealed part of myself. I moved on with life. I was the leader, the innovator, executive director, the funder, community engagement specialist, activist, and the proudest feminist man in Miami. I was changing the culture of misogyny one man at a time.

One afternoon in mid-February, I was walking to my nine-to-five gig when I received a call from the newly elected commissioner of Miami, Ken Russell. He told me that he wanted to select me as the first man to serve on the Miami Commission for the status of women. I was shocked and really not interested because I never wanted to be around politicians. I told him I was honored, but I didn't know anything about Miami politics. He said that I was doing a respectable job already for women in the city and was more than qualified to serve on the board. I didn't believe it because this was not in my vision. I had a vision of building a big army of men to support the women's empowerment movement, but this historic appointment was not one of them. My last words to him were, "Thank you, and I am honored to serve."

The day after we spoke, he made the announcement via the City of Miami social media page. On February 24, 2016, I made history. I became an American pioneer. I was the first man appointed to the commission of the status of women in Miami, one of the most glamorous and unequal cities in the world. Miami is the second-worst city in the U.S. for income and poverty level. Roughly 15 percent of the population lives below poverty. Social and economic inequality is as severe in Miami as many South American countries.

The next thing I noticed was that I was getting friend requests from people who were politically involved in the community. I was happy to connect with them because I was no longer underground building the movement. I was getting the attention of all the concerned residents of Miami, black, white, and yellow. I connected and learned from them. Meanwhile, the status quo wasn't very happy about my historic appointment. Their agenda was to keep black people impoverished in Miami by marginalizing them politically, silencing and persecuting black leaders, and dividing the people. That's their devilish strategy to keep black people in their place at the bottom of the socioeconomic ladder. Through their private foundations and Cuban politicians, they control the lifeblood of the people.

Around the time of my appointment, Bernie Sanders was rallying and leading the 2016 presidential race. He was going against the millionaire and billionaire class who was buying politicians and corrupting the U.S. democratic experiment. He was speaking about the real issues - healthcare for all, education reform, and income inequality. During his campaign, he said, "It doesn't make sense that the top 1% owns almost as much wealth as the bottom 90%." The corporate media, which is owned by the top 1%, didn't care about real issues or substance in the 2016 presidential election. They completely ignored Bernie's campaign and other sane Republican candidates, like John Kasich. Instead, they gave Donald Trump more than 1 billion dollars of free media to turn the presidential election into a reality TV show. The top 1% percent Bernie was talking about wanted Hillary to win the presidential election. They knew her only shot was through a candidate like Donald Trump. I was disgusted by the presidential election. It was the whitest presidential race ever. Fear and hate were the two most powerful emotions being released. I couldn't wait for the election, or selection, to be over.

Meanwhile, I noticed black men were getting shot almost every other day by the white establishment. I used to ride around in a scooter. I put it on the side and used shared transportation systems like Lyft and Uber. I was being watched, and I didn't want to be targeted and get shot like so many black men across the country. I felt alone, but fearless.

The Miami establishment was standing in front of me. I was paying attention to every move the Obama administration made. I trusted

President Obama's leadership and judgment. I believed in him and his vision for the future. Our stories are different, but somehow I knew we were going to meet to birth this new freedom on this earth. When his administration announced the launching of the "first-ever White House summit in the United States of Women" in early May, they called on many community leaders working on improving the status of women across the country. I saw it on Facebook. I nominated myself and asked a few of my friends to nominate me as well.

On May 18, 2016, the most important day in black history, I received an email stating that I had been nominated to attend the United States of Women hosted by the White House on June 14th! I couldn't believe it. I was surprised not just by the nomination, but also by the date. May 18 is one of the most celebrated days in Haitian culture. It's the decisive day when General Jean-Jacques Dessalines ripped the white portion of the French flag and sewed the red and blue as a symbolic gesture in the war against France and European colonialism. It was also a symbol of union between blacks and the mixed-race population, which was called *mulattoes*. I was at my office in the government building when I received the email. When I got home, I posted it on my Facebook wall.

The summit was held in Washington from June 14- 15. The day I left Miami to attend the conference in Washington, DC, I received two friend requests from the president of the Knight Foundation; one on Facebook and the other on LinkedIn. I was a little shocked and nervous, knowing the history of racial terrorism in this country. I also remembered when I first met him back in 2010. He brought up Hillary's name out of nowhere when I shared my idea with him on improving U.S. democracy. I told him that I believed women are finer and morally superior to men and that if we invest in them, U.S. democracy will be better. Now that Hillary was running a soulless campaign and I had emerged as a champion for women's rights in the city, I got a friend request from him on social media. I accepted the LinkedIn friend request right away, but not the Facebook one. I waited until I got to Washington to accept the Facebook friend request.

The energy of the country was positive and uplifting. There were thousands of poto mitan from across the country at the summit. Poto mitan is a term used to describe women as the pillars of society. There was a new air of freedom in the conference. All the bathrooms were gender neutral. Everyone was talking and getting to know each other. All the four colors foretold by Indigenous elders of Turtle Island (America) were there. Black, white, yellow, and red people. There was a working harmony. I didn't feel the colonial spirit in the conference or the spirit of arrogance and fear.

First Lady Michelle Obama and Oprah were the inspiring speakers. During the two-day conference, I didn't see or hear from Hillary Clinton. I was amazed by her spirit of arrogance. I didn't want to believe a woman could be this arrogant and feel entitled. She didn't attend this historic summit nor send a video message asking all the grassroots leaders for support when they went back home to their respective communities. She felt entitled to the throne. From that moment, I realized she was going to be selected by the corporate establishment. I realized that racist billionaires run America.

When I got back to Miami, I decided to accept Mr. Alberto Ibargüen's Facebook request and send him this message privately: "Hi, Mr. Alberto. I feel flattered to be connected with you on social media. I didn't know what to think when I received your friend request. If your schedule permits, will you be interested in meeting with me in the upcoming weeks? I would like to get your support for a BIG community event in October to raise awareness of domestic violence." He replied with this message: "Hello, Christian. I sent a friend request because you popped up on my FB page and seemed to be doing interesting things. Your project sounds outside of our funding focus, but I would encourage you to reach out to Matt Haggman, our Miami program office at H****@knightfoundation.org. I am traveling for Knight or with my family from now until past Labor Day, but perhaps in the fall we can share a cup of coffee. Thanks for writing. Alberto."

I replied, "Thanks for the instant reply. I will reach out to Matt. Have a wonderful time with your family. I look forward to sharing a cup of coffee with you."

After this brief exchange, I said to myself, "I didn't ask the guy for funding. Why did he bring funding in the conversation?" When he said we can share a cup of coffee in the fall, I interpreted it as after the 2016 presidential election. He is a powerful member of the status quo. As a son of Haiti, I knew what he meant when he mentioned Hillary after I told him that investing in U.S. women would advance American democracy.

I was looking forward to sharing a cup of coffee with him because at the time it looked like Hillary was going to win. Major white platforms were supporting her. Fashion magazines, such as Vogue, were behind her. CNN was unapologetically standing and celebrating her victory before the result. The status quo made it obvious that Hillary was going to win.

President Obama even mentioned it in his last corresponding dinner in 2016. He said jokingly, "Next year at this time, someone else will be standing here in this very spot, and it's anyone's guess who she will be."

Being almost certain Hillary Clinton was going to be called "Madam President," I featured mostly white men in the 2016 DADE MEN exhibit than the previous ones. I told them the reason I was leading this movement to raise men's awareness of gender-based violence was for many reasons. First, I was inspired by my mother; second, I wanted to build a leadership academy for girls in Haiti. In the 2016 DADE MEN Photography exhibition, there wasn't a big crowd like the one I hosted in 2015. Millions were disbursed by the white foundations to distract the movement. BME was hosting an event the same day, and every other leader who was getting a grant from the Miami establishment was advised not to attend. Only a few people attended. I was satisfied anyway because I wanted to let the Miami establishment know that I am going to build this movement whether they like it or not. Whether Hillary wins or not.

I doubted Hillary was going to win when I started to notice she wasn't attracting millennials. Her campaign was all about fear and arrogance. Trump's was about hate, arrogance, and fear. The best speeches during her campaign were delivered by First Lady Michelle Obama. At the Democratic National Convention, Hillary was dull and soulless. When the white press leaked the video of Donald Trump bragging about sexually assaulting married women on October 7, 2016, Hillary didn't take a stand for those white women. She asked First Lady Michelle Obama to speak on her behalf. I didn't want to believe that. I didn't want to believe the woman who was selected by the white establishment could not defend herself and women who look like her.

At that point, I left everything in God's hand. One thing I knew for sure, I was going to vote for her. A part of me wanted her to win because I thought it would have been a symbolic victory for white women. Another part of me believes she would have unleashed the darkest side of the feminine and strengthen the spirit of misogyny. I left everything in God's hand. I already felt that I was in God's hand. I wasn't worried.

The Miami establishment gave a grant to another group of "black" leaders to host a "Brave Man Breakfast" in Little Haiti a few weeks before the 2016 presidential result. A few days after, Hillary made a surprise visit to little Haiti with Trayvon Martin's mother a day before the election to lie to the Haitian people just like Donald Trump did a month before. At this point, I was an watching the workings of colonial patriarchy and democracy. All the black men who attended this "Brave Man Breakfast" were recipients of the Knight Foundation through the BME organization.

When the result came in on November 9, 2016, the former reality television star, Donald Trump, was elected the next president of the United States. All of a sudden, darkness fell across the Americas and the world. Young women all over the country were disappointed and in tears. Hillary was expecting to win so badly. She couldn't even give a concession speech that night. She delivered her best speech throughout the whole campaign the day after she lost.

With Trump being president-elect, my work became a little easier because most women who classify themselves as feminists didn't fully understand the work that I was doing. Now, I was waiting to share a cup of coffee with Mr. Alberto from the Knight Foundation. He was in charge of a powerful white institution in the country, and he thought I was doing interesting work in the city, so I was patiently waiting for an email or private message on social media to share a cup of coffee. I waited for days, weeks, and months and didn't hear from him.

The next year, at the annual event they titled " PAMM Fund for African American Art," I went to find him to remind him about our meeting in the fall. When we saw each other, he gave me a soft handshake and said as he walked away, "I am going to invest in black men." That statement convinced me then he was a professional, committed, and covert racist.

After our re-encounter on February 2017, he kept sending me subliminal racist messages through "leaders" he controlled in Little Haiti. At that time, Miami-Dade County government was not interested in the partnership anymore. They weren't interested in having a conversation about domestic violence and sexual assault in the city. I was gently kicked out of the office because I didn't have insurance for the building.

Seeing the world quickly changing faces, the UN-appointed António Guterres, an old white man from Portugal on January 1, 2017. Ironically, Portugal is the European country that initiated the kidnapping of African children to be sold as slaves in the New World. The Clinton Foundation pulled out of Haiti, and I knew then that Haiti needed to get back on the stage of history to shed light. Somehow, these archaic and deeply wounded white men were going to insult our spirits.

For DADE MEN 2017, I recruited mostly black men. I learned from the Haitian warriors and my black American family that white men cannot be fully trusted because they have been marinated in a racist culture and also because their privileges are injuries to black and Indigenous people of the land. Instead of hosting the DADE MEN photography exhibit on October 1, 2017, I put the event together on the eve of International Men's Day, November 18, 2017. The same night, the white press announced via their propaganda machine that black human beings were being sold as slaves in Libya.

After DADE MEN 2017, the president of the Knight Foundation used one of his workers, aka black leaders, to invite me to the Knight Foundation's yearly gathering. I meditated and prayed about it. I didn't want to meet him anymore. I didn't feel good about him. Then a friend told me to go and meet with him. When I did, he didn't use the word "black" at all. He approached me and shook my hand softly again. In a spirit of arrogance and white power, he asked me to email him so he can introduce me to Trabian Shorter whom he had given six million dollars. I was with a friend. I asked him, "Why do you think the first thing he told me was the amount of money he gave to the guy. Was he trying to impress me? Does he actually think six million dollars is a lot of money to me? He probably doesn't know I am my ancestors re-incarnated."

My last DADE MEN in 2018 was disrupted. I held a prayer ceremony with some of the men. We prayed for women all over the world. For years, I have tried to write this memoir, and I was unable to. I couldn't put words down. My mind and spirit were heading in opposite directions. I wanted to tell the story from an academic perspective, but the story is a spirit-led story. I have been following my spirit and the spirit of my ancestors since September 11, 1988. I realized throughout my journey from Haiti to the United States that I was always being guided by my ancestral fire. I was never walking alone. It was by divine order that an exceptional mother and loving woman raised me. It was by divine order that she was impregnated during a one-night stand in Haiti by my father. As scriptures say, "Before I formed you in the womb I knew you, and before you were born I set you apart; I appointed you as a prophet to the nations."

My historic appointment on February 24, 2016 was by divine order. I don't want to sound blasphemous, but I feel in every core of my being that the great spirit sent me to Turtle Island (North America) to share the good news to all the American people. Blacks, whites, yellows, reds.

The best days of the United States are ahead of her, but first, Euro-Americans must admit that they committed great sins against God's children. Euro-Americans have committed great sins against the peaceful and loving Indigenous people of the land. They must heal relations with them first, not with black people.

The great spirit has sent me to help in the healing process and to remind all good Americans to come together for the sake of the American republic. To remind them of the words of an exceptional American politician and two great American prophets: Abraham Lincoln, Frederick Douglass, and Martin Luther King, Jr. They have all warned the American people about the time we are living in.

On November 19, 1863, four and half months after the Union armies defeated the Confederate Army at the Battle of Gettysburg, President Abraham Lincoln echoed his prophecy to future generations. "The brave men, living and dead, who struggled here, have consecrated it, far above our poor power to add or detract. The world will little note, nor long remember what we say here. It is for us the living, rather, to be dedicated here to the unfinished work which they who fought here have thus far so nobly advanced. It is rather for us to be here dedicated to the great task remaining before us... that from these honored dead we take increased devotion to that cause for which they gave the last full measure of devotion.. that we here highly resolve that these dead shall not have died in vain... that this nation, under God, shall have a new freedom.. and that government of the people, by the people, for the people, shall not perish from the earth."

On January 2, 1893, thirty years after President Lincoln's Gettysburg Address, the great Frederick Douglass was selected by the Haitian government to speak to Euro-Americans at the World's Columbian Exposition held in Chicago to celebrate the 400th anniversary of Christopher Columbus' arrival in 1492 and colonization of the "New World." Frederick Douglass told the audience, "Haiti is a rich country. She has many things which we need, and we have many things which she needs. Intercourse between us is easy. Measuring distance by time and improved steam navigation, Haiti will one day be only three days from New York and thirty-six hours from Florida; in fact, our next-door neighbor. On this account, as well as others equally important, friendly and helpful, relations should subsist between the two countries. Though we have a thousand years of civilization behind us, and Haiti only a century behind her; though we are large, and Haiti is small; though we are strong, and Haiti is weak; though we are a continent and Haiti is bounded on all sides by the sea, there may come a time when even in the weakness of Haiti there may be strength to the United States."_

On April 3, 1968, the day before Dr. King would be assassinated, he delivered his last speech on earth, "I Have Been to the Mountaintop" at the Mason Temple (Church of God in Christ Headquarters) in Memphis. Unfortunately, very few people have heard, read, and meditated on his message well. He spoke as if he knew the day was his last. He said, "Men, for years now, have been talking about war and peace. But now, no longer can they just talk about it. It is no longer a choice between violence and nonviolence in this world. It's nonviolence or nonexistence that is where we are today. And also in the human rights revolution, if something isn't done, and done in a hurry, to bring the colored peoples of the world out of their long years of poverty, their long years of hurt and neglect, the entire world is doomed."_

Those three exceptional men in their own ways have shifted American society from a slave-holding democracy and racial tyranny to the task we have in front of us today - this great possibility of ushering in a new birth of freedom on this Earth. Like President Obama said 2013, "It remains the task of us all, as citizens of these United States, to be the authors of the next great chapter in our American story." But to write this chapter gloriously and properly, we have to listen to women who are from the four directions of the world. They are all carrying medicine for our "collective healing" as my Indigenous brothers and sisters believe and wisdom for our journeys. At the Nobel Women's Initiative Conference in 2009, a group of women issued this extraordinary statement that I believe every man should read and meditate upon:

"We call upon all states and multilateral institutions to recognize that the democratization process is incomplete and does not end with elections. No country or society can claim to be democratic when the women who form half its citizens are denied their right to life, to their human rights and entitlements, and to safety and security. Despite this, we women have made extraordinary efforts to democratize the institutions of society that frame our lives and the well-being of all humanity-- the family, the community, clan, tribe, ethnic or religious group, political, legal, economic, social and cultural structures, and the media and communications systems. But our search for justice is continually overwhelmed by the violence perpetrated upon us, by the exploitation and colonization of our bodies, our labor, and our lands, by militarization, war, and civil conflict; by persistent and increasing poverty; and by environmental degradation. All of these forces affect us, and our children, far more severely and in unique ways. We know that democracy that comes from the heart and is not rule of the majority, but the safeguards with equal rights fosters a culture of peace. We are in search of democracy that transforms not just our lives, but all society -- and we will not be silenced until it is achieved in every part of the world."

"We are living in a time of great danger and great possibility." Collectively, we have more power now to begin the world over again than when Thomas Paine uttered this slogan centuries ago. We have more opportunity and human capital to start brand new institutions to end the world's oldest tyranny, poverty. Poverty coupled with ignorance has caused more suffering in the world than all the major conflict throughout our history combined. I firmly believe when healing of the races become trendy, and gender equality becomes a national security issue in the developed world, we will make poverty history. We will begin to restore beauty and harmony on Mother Earth. The choice is ours. The world has shrunk into a global village.

Our generation can do more with less. If each generation must discover its mission, fulfill it, or betray it in relative opacity as Frantz Fanon believed. Then the mission of our generation is to elevate women and advocate for their wellbeing and safety. For us to accomplish this mission, we have to erect a new type of man. Dr. King believed this new man is the non-violent man that he gloriously embodied.

I believe this new man is the Indigenous man, the Haytian man, as Dessalines and the Haytian heroes instructed us "to be worthy of being a Haytian, you have to be a good son, a good husband, a good father, a good citizen, and most importantly a good warrior." Although I was not fully aware of the sacred instructions my ancestors left me, I always carried them in my genetic memory. My spirit was always yearning to be like Emperor Jean-Jacques Dessalines. His mission was to avenge America. Mine is to help heal it.

I am excited about this moment in time. Too many ancestors have died, bled, shed tears, and prayed for this moment in history for us to play small. We must begin a new history of man. In the wretched of the earth, Frantz Fanon wrote, "If we want to transform Africa into a new Europe, America, then let us entrust the destinies of our countries to the Europeans. They will do a better job than the rest of us. But if we want humanity to take one step forward, if we want to take it to another level than the one where Europe has placed it, then we must innovate, we must be pioneers." We are at this critical moment right now in history where humanity must take one step forward.

I am not sure the written words are sufficient to help us leap. Emotions are too high for most of the white population. They have been indoctrinated with the myth of racial superiority and blinded by prejudices for 500 years. I am not sure the Clinton's generation is ready to leap. They are too marinated in the racist culture of the old and dying America. The new America is being held hostage by the billionaire class as Bernie Sanders always points out. The truth of the matter is billionaires, nor politicians cannot save us. We the people can only save ourselves.

International institutions, such as the United Nations, world banks, and the Organization of American States have deceived and failed us. They are all European organizations and thus have colonial projects that have one mission : To enslave black and brown nations. We are living in a time of exposure as Sherry Mitchell noted in her book, *The Sacred Instructions*, "where the light of truth is shining into all the dark corners of our lives and our world. I do not know nor have any new truth to reveal as to what we must do. What I know for sure is individual and collective healing is critical to our survival as a species. I am relying on the spirit and the wisdom of the ancestors get me through. This is why I often use their words and wisdom. They are men and women who have survived and thrived some of the darkest chapters of colonial history for this grand opportunity. As Emperor Halie Selassie asked during his historic address to the United Nations in 1963, "Where are we to look for our survival, for the answers to the questions which have never before been posed? We must look, first, to Almighty God, who has raised man above the animals and endowed him intelligence and reason. We must put faith in Him, that He will not desert us or permit us to destroy humanity which He created in His image. And we must look into ourselves, into the depth of our souls. We must become something we have never been and for which our education and experience and environment have ill-prepared us. We must become bigger than we have been; more courageous, greater in spirit, larger in outlook. We must become members of a new race, overcoming petty prejudice, owing our ultimate allegiance not nations but to our fellow men within the human community." Or in other words, we must become better men and women. That begins with the decolonization of our minds, bodies, and spirits. We must learn how to live as a family or perish as fools. It will start with teaching boys and men how to respect, honor, and support women and elders. As the Indigenous elders say, "Men do not have power. They have responsibilities. Women have power." Our most sacred responsibility is to defend women and Mother Earth. It is time for us learn how to be good and respectful men. Now it's time for white-skinned people to renounce their arrogance and greed to seek healing from the Indigenous people of the Americas."

To quote Frantz Fanon, "Come, comrades, the European game is finally over. We must look for something else." On a personal note, when I look deeply and honestly at the way my journey is unfolding, I realize that I always followed the sacred instructions of my ancestors and honored the sacred oath taken at Gonaives on January 1, 1804. I am doing exactly what my ancestors told me to do. "I prostrate myself in grateful humility at the feet of the eternal and return to him unnumbered thanks: I admire the wisdom of his designs and the impenetrable methods which he has employed to deliver the oppressed and chastise the oppressors." In conclusion of this memoir, I want to share a poem that I think describes my journey beautifully from a slum in Port-au-Prince in Haiti to becoming a women's rights champion and a pioneer.

Epilogue

"When nature wants to make a man, and shake a man, and wake a man;
When nature wants to make a man to do the future's will;
When she tries with all her skill
And she yearns with all her soul to create him large and whole...
With what cunning she prepares him!
How she goads and never spares him!
How she whets him, and frets him, and poverty begets him...
How she often disappoints
How she often anoints,
With what wisdom she will hide him,
Never minding what betide him, though his genius sob with slighting
And his pride may not forget !
Bids him struggle harder yet.
Makes him lonely
So that only
God's high message shall reach him,
So that she may surely teach him what the hierarchy planned.
Though he may not understand
Gives him passions to command.
How remorselessly she spurs him
With terrific ardor stirs him
When she poignantly prefers him.
Lo, the crisis ! Lo the shout
That must call the leader out.
When the people need salvation
Doth he come to lead the Nation
Then doth Nature show her plan when the world has found- A MAN."

Bibliography

1. Julia Garfield. *The Haitian Declaration of Independence: Creation, Context, and Legacy (UVA, 2016) pages 239-247*

2. Boisrond-Tonnerre. *Mémoires pour servir a L'histoire D' Haïti (1851, edited by Saint- Rémy Joseph, Paris France Libraire)*

3. Marcus Rainsford. *A Historical Account of the Black Empire of Hayti (Duke University Press Durham and London 2013)*

4. Toussaint L'ouverture. *A lecture by Wendel Phillips (1861, toussaintLouverture.org)*

5. Baron De Vastey. *An Essay on the causes of the revolution and civil wars of Hayti. (Translated from French by W.H.M.B 1823, www.forgottenbooks.com)*

6. Marcus Garvey. *Ultimate collection of speeches and poems*

7. Marleine L Daut. *Tropics of Haiti (2015, Liverpool University Press) pages 84-85*

8. Baron De Vastey. *The colonial system unveiled (translated from French by Chris Bongie 2009, Liverpool University Press)*

9. Rethinking Columbus: *The next 500 years (edited by Bill Bigelow and Bob Peterson, 2nd edition 1998)*

10. Valerie M. Hudson, Bonnie Ballif-Spanvill, Mary Caprioli, Chad F. Emmett. *Sex and World Peace (Columbia University Press, New York 2012) pages 71, 154,155.*

11. Steven Pinker. *The better angels of our nature: How violence has declined (2012, Penguin books) pages*

12. Sherri Mitchell- Weh'na Ha'mu Kwasset. *The sacred instructions (2018, North Atlantic Books)*

13. Howard Zinn. *A People's History of the United States (1999, HarperCollins Publishers) Pages 346-347*

14. The Haitian Pavillion. *Lecture on Haiti by Frederick Douglass (1893, Chicago world's Fair)*

15. Bill Clinton. *My life (2004, Random House, Inc., New York)*

16. Hillary Clinton. *Hard choices (2014, Simon & Schuster)*

17. George W Bush. *Decision points (2010, broadway Paperbacks, an imprint of the Crown Publishing Group.)*

THE MIAMI FOUNDATION
200 SOUTH BISCAYNE BOULEVARD, SUITE 505
MIAMI FL 33131-5330

011777

To: Millennials Project, Inc

10/2/2014

INVOICE NUMBER	DATE	DESCRIPTION	AMOUNT	DISCOUNT	NET AMOUNT
GE-DA-14-23941-1	10/2/2014	KNIG - The John S. & James L. Knight Foundation Fund	$5,000.00	$0.00	$5,000.00
		Totals:	**$5,000.00**	**$0.00**	**$5,000.00**

MEMORANDUM OF UNDERSTANDING
BETWEEN NEW SMILES FOUNDATION, INC. AND MIAMI-DADE COUNTY, COMMUNITY ACTION AND HUMAN SERVICES DEPARTMENT

This Memorandum of Understanding (hereinafter "MOU") is made and entered into this 25th day of September 2014 by **Millennials Project** (hereinafter "Partner") and Miami-Dade County, Community Action and Human Services Department, a political subdivision of the State of Florida (hereinafter "County").

RECITALS

WHEREAS, pursuant to Resolution 1372-04, the Board of County Commissioners (the "Board") requested the development of both a comprehensive study of the existing service delivery for victims of domestic violence and sexual assault and an appropriate improvement plan; and

WHEREAS, in September 2005, the result of the study was presented to the Board and the report indicated that although there are very valuable victim services available in the community through both the public sector and private, not-for-profit, community-based Partners, these services are not integrated in a manner to maximize efficiency and ease of accessibility for clients; and

WHEREAS, the County Manager, through Resolution 1086-05, was directed to implement a comprehensive system involving the full spectrum of services available in the community; and

WHEREAS, the County Manager directed the Department of Human Services to prepare a plan for the coordination of victim services by establishing a Coordinated Victims Assistance Center ("CVAC") where service providers would be co-located; and

WHEREAS, in December 2007, pursuant to Resolution 1302-07, the County purchased a building, located at 2400 South Dixie Highway, Miami, Florida 33133, for the purpose of establishing the Coordinated Victims Assistance Center (hereinafter "CVAC"); and

WHEREAS, Miami-Dade County recognizes the synergistic value of networking and collaboration in public/private initiatives involving government agencies, community-based organizations, health and human services providers, and law enforcement; and

WHEREAS, Miami-Dade County is desirous of providing victims of domestic violence and sexual assault with greater access to enhanced and coordinated services through multidisciplinary collaboration in one location to include: victim-centered advocacy and other collateral support services that will facilitate the achievement of peace and safety for victims and their children; and

WHEREAS, the Partner is committed to working to make the CVAC a successful resource for the residents of Miami-Dade County; and

WHEREAS, the Miami-Dade County Board of County Commissioners, at its October 7, 2008 meeting, has authorized executing an MOU with the Partner;

NOW THEREFORE, in consideration of the premises and mutual covenants and promises contained herein, the County and the Partner agree as follows:

ARTICLE I
PURPOSE

The Purpose of this MOU is to memorialize the relationship with the Partner and with Miami-Dade County to ensure the success of the CVAC for Miami-Dade County residents who are victims of domestic violence and sexual assault.

ARTICLE II
TERM OF THE MOU

The term of this MOU shall be one (1) year from the date of execution by the parties unless terminated by either party pursuant to Article VII below. This Agreement may be renewed on an annual basis at the option of the County and by agreement between the parties.

2.2 The parties agree that time is of the essence in the performance of each and every obligation under this MOU.

ARTICLE III
RESPONSIBILITIES OF THE PARTIES

3.1 Partner Responsibilities. The Partner hereby agrees as follows:

a. The Chief Executive Officer of the **Millennials Project** and/or designee, will establish and maintain a working relationship and a principal point of contact with the County.

b. The Chief Executive Officer of the **Millennials Project, or** designee, will provide general non identifying aggregate reports as needed with regard to the clients assisted by the agency at the CVAC.

c. The **Millennials Project** will, to the extent allowed by Florida Law, Federal Law, share information with the County.

d. The **Millennials Project** will agree to participate in on site partner meetings and training sessions as applicable

e. The **Millennials Project** agrees to conduct its operations and activities in accordance with a mission statement, purpose goals, and objectives that are consistent with that of the County and of CVAC.

f. The **Millennials Project** agrees to collaborate in efforts to secure funding that promotes the mission statement of the CVAC when practicable.

By: MILLENIALS PROJECT

Christian Guerrier
CEO

By: COMMUNITY ACTION AND HUMAN SERVICES DEPARTMENT

Lucia Davis-Raiford, Director

ATTEST:
Harvey Ruvin, Clerk

Deputy Clerk

COUNTY COMMISSIONERS MIAMI-DADE COUNTY FLORIDA

MIAMI-DADE COUNTY, FLORIDA
BY ITS BOARD OF
COUNTY COMMISSIONERS

By:
for Carlos A. Gimenez
Mayor

200 South Biscayne Boulevard
Suite 505
Miami, FL 33131-5330
305.371.2711
miamifoundation.org

October 3, 2014

Mr. Christian Guerrier
President and Founder
Millennials Project, Inc.
2400 South Dixie Highway
Miami, FL 33133

Dear Mr. Guerrier:

Enclosed you will find grant check number 11777 in the amount of $5,000.00. **This grant has been made possible by the Knight Foundation Fund at The Miami Foundation.** This grant is for programming that promotes healthy manhood to help prevent domestic violence, sexual assault, bullying and homophobia.

This distribution is being made to you based on a recommendation The Miami Foundation received from the John S. and James L. Knight Foundation's Program Director for Miami, Matt Haggman. No tickets, merchandise or benefits resulting in private inurement are to be issued to the donor as a result of this gift.

In receiving this grant, you and your organization agree to:

- Make reference to the **"Knight Foundation Fund at The Miami Foundation"** when acknowledging this grant in your literature.
- Contact Knight Foundation's Communications Director Anusha Alikhan, alikhan@knightfoundation.org before making any public announcement.
- Refer to knightcommunications.org for tips on writing releases and communicating about Knight. There you can find the Knight Foundation boilerplate, which should be included in your release, along with style guidelines.

The Miami Foundation is pleased to be able to support your organization through its philanthropic fund program.

If you have any questions, please do not hesitate to call.

Sincerely,

Pamela Olmo

Pamela Olmo
VP, Finance and CFO

PO/cd

Enclosure

cc: Mr. Matt Haggman

City of Miami

February 24, 2016

Mr. Christian Guerrier
Millennials Project
2400 South Dixie Highway
Miami, Florida 33133

Dear Mr. Guerrier:

Congratulations on your recent appointment to the Miami Commission of the Status of Women ("MCSW"). On behalf of the entire Board, I'd like to welcome you to our board and invite you to our next meeting to be held on Wednesday, March 2, 2016, at 6:00 p.m. – Miami City Hall, City Manager's Conference Room – 2nd Floor. Our meetings are held on the first Wednesday of each month (except August) from 6:00 p.m. – 7:30 p.m. at Miami City Hall, Staff Room, unless otherwise noticed.

As a member of the MCSW, you are required to attend an Ethics training provided through the Office of the City Clerk at times announced by the City Clerk. You will be advised of the next scheduled training.

Enclosed for your information is relevant information pertaining to the scope of the function of the MCSW, as well as the current membership roster. Also enclosed is a DRAFT copy of the board's last minutes to familiarize you with our current activities.

Should you require additional information, or have any questions feel free to contact me or Angela Roberts, MCSW Staff Liaison at the telephone number listed herein, or via email aroberts@miamigov.com.

Again, congratulations on your appointment. We look forward to working with you.

A Roberts
for Allyson Warren, Chairperson
Miami Commission of the Status of Women

MIAMI COMMISSION ON THE STATUS OF WOMEN
444 S.W. 2nd Avenue, Room 642 / Miami, Florida 33130 / (305) 416-1990 / Fax: (305) 416-1995

Miami Commission on the Status of Women

Agenda
March 2, 2016
6:00pm
CITY HALL – CITY MANAGER'S CONFERENCE ROOM

1. Call to Order

2. Roll Call

3. Approval of minutes from February 3, 2016

4. Discussion of new business:

   MCSW Breakfast

   (FYI) Reminder: Annual Report Oral Presentation – March 11, 2016

5. Next Meeting: April 6, 2016

6. Adjournment

MILLENNIALS PROJECT

AMONG US MEN MEETING

Thursday, February 5, 2015

AGENDA

Welcome……………………………………………………Christian Guerrier Jr, Founder & CEO
The Millennials Project

Self-Introductions……………………………………………………………………All Attendees

Hip Hop: Beyond rhymes & beats ……………………………………………………A 2006 documentary film produced by Byron Hurt on masculinity, violence, homophobia and sexism in hip hop music and culture.

Dialogue…………………………………………………………………………………………

Millennials Project is a 501(c3)non profit organization dedicated to help end all forms of violence against women and girls.

OMB Number: 1122-0020
Expiration Date: 8/31/2015

U.S. Department of Justice
Office on Violence Against Women (OVW)

OVW Fiscal Year 2015 Consolidated Grant Program to Address Children and Youth Experiencing Domestic and Sexual Assault and Engage Men and Boys as Allies

Solicitation

Solicitation Release Date

This solicitation was released on or about February 6, 2015.

Eligibility

Applicants are limited to:

1. A nonprofit, nongovernmental entity with **either**:
   - A. a demonstrated primary goal of providing services to children or youth who are victims of and/or exposed to sexual assault, domestic violence, dating violence, or stalking; **OR**
   - B. a primary goal of serving adult victims of sexual assault, domestic violence, dating violence, or stalking, but which has a demonstrated history of providing comprehensive services to children or youth who are victims of and/or exposed to sexual assault, domestic violence, dating violence, sexual assault, or stalking; **OR**
   - C. a demonstrated history of creating effective public education and/or community organizing campaigns to encourage men and boys to work as allies with women and girls to prevent sexual assault, domestic violence, dating violence, and stalking;

DUNS #
SAM

OMB Number: 1122-0020
Expiration Date: 8/31/2015

2. An Indian tribe or tribal nonprofit organization that provides services to children and youth who are victims of and/or exposed to sexual assault, domestic violence, dating violence, or stalking; **or**
3. A territorial, tribal or unit of local government entity.

(See "Eligibility")

Deadlines

Application: All applications are due by 11:59 p.m. Eastern Time (E.T.) on March 19, 2015.
(See "Submission Dates and Times")

Registration: To ensure all applicants have ample time to complete the registration process, applicants must obtain a Data Universal Number System (DUNS) Number, register online with the System for Award Management (SAM) and with **Grants.gov** immediately, but no later than February 26, 2015.

(See "Registration")

Letter of Registration: Applicants are strongly encouraged to submit a letter of registration to **ovw.consolyouth@usdoj.gov** by February 26, 2015. This will ensure that applicants are well-positioned to successfully submit an application by the deadline. This letter will not obligate potential applicants to submit an application. Interested applicants who do not submit a Letter of Registration are still eligible to apply.

(See "Letter of Registration")

Pre-Application Conference Calls: OVW will conduct Pre-Application Conference Calls for anyone interested in submitting an application for the **Consolidated Youth Program.** Participation in these calls is optional. Interested applicants who do not participate are still eligible to apply.

(See "Content and Form of Application Submission")

Contact Information

For assistance with the requirements of this solicitation, contact OVW at (202) 307-6026.

In Fiscal Year 2015, OVW applications will be submitted through Grants.gov. For technical assistance with Grants.gov, contact the Grants.gov Customer Support Hotline at 1-800-518-4726.

Grants.gov Number assigned to announcement **OVW-2015-4046.**

It is anticipated that all applicants will be notified of the outcome of their applications by September 30, 2015.

Oh, Great Spirit,
whose voice I hear in the winds
and whose breath gives life to all the world, hear me.
I am small and weak.
I need your strength and wisdom.

Let me walk in beauty and make my eyes
ever behold the red and purple sunset.
Make my hands respect the things you have made
and my ears sharp to hear your voice.
Make me wise so that I may understand
the things you have taught my people.
Let me learn the lessons you have hidden
in every leaf and rock.

I seek strength, not to be superior to my brother,
but to fight my greatest enemy - myself.
Make me always ready to come to you
with clean hands and straight eyes,
so when life fades, as the fading sunset,
my spirit will come to you
without shame.

Yellow Lark, Lakota

Millennials Project
invites you to

DADE MEN

**THE PHOTOGRAPHY EXHIBIT
TO RAISE AWARENESS ON
DOMESTIC VIOLENCE**

**Saturday,
November 18, 2017
7 pm - 11 pm**

1074 N.W. 3rd Avenue,
Miami Fl 33136

Music by Dj Tillery James & special performance by world class violinist, Guy A. Michel.

ALL PROCEEDS WILL SUPPORT
GIRLS EDUCATION IN HAITI.

EARLY BIRD $25 / DOOR $50
for info about tickets, visit www.millennialsproject.org

Photography by Dante' Diaskos Filyau

Made in USA - Kendallville, IN
99745_9780578586496
09 12.2022 1259